Moulton College

NORTHAMPTONSHIRE

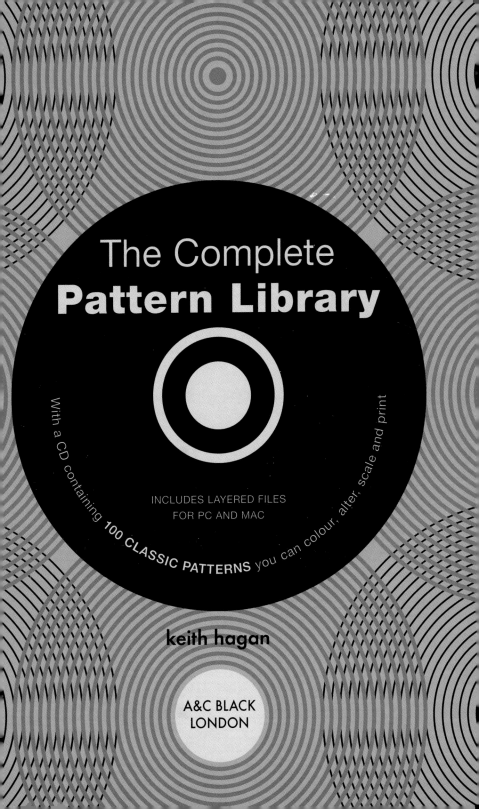

The Complete
Pattern Library

With a CD containing **100 CLASSIC PATTERNS** you can colour, alter, scale and print

INCLUDES LAYERED FILES
FOR PC AND MAC

keith hagan

A&C BLACK
LONDON

First published in 2005 by
A&C BLACK PUBLISHERS LIMITED
37 Soho Square
London W1D 3QZ
www.acblack.com

ISBN-10: 0-7136-7254-4

ISBN-13: 978-0-7136-7254-1

A CIP catalogue record is available from the British Library.

Cover design by Sutchinda Thompson

This book was created by
THE IVY PRESS LIMITED
The Old Candlemakers
West Street, Lewes
East Sussex BN7 2NZ

PUBLISHER Sophie Collins
CREATIVE DIRECTOR Peter Bridgewater
EDITORIAL DIRECTOR Jason Hook
DESIGN MANAGER Simon Goggin
SENIOR PROJECT EDITOR Caroline Earle
DESIGNER Richard Constable
ILLUSTRATOR Adam Elliott at Verus Design
INTRODUCTORY TEXT Adam Juniper

Printed and bound in China

Contents

Introduction

Patterns, by their very nature, repeat at intervals that can be described mathematically. Computers think of everything, even images, in terms of mathematics, and *The Complete Pattern Library* exploits this fact to enable you to create an infinite variety of patterns using your computer. It consists of a book illustrating patterns from the history of design, and a CD with the same patterns in image files that you can use on your computer.

The computer is a fantastic creative tool, allowing you to scale a pattern – and change its colours or even reconfigure it – in a matter of moments. Your pattern can be repeated with perfect accuracy in a few steps, so you can get on with whatever you're creating, be it a T-shirt, a book cover or a website.

The patterns included on the disk are compatible with either Apple Mac or PC.

You can open the pattern files on the CD included with this book with virtually any modern computer, whether it's Apple Macintosh or Microsoft Windows. The key is to use software that can read the file formats provided. We've tried to make that easy by including every pattern in the common EPS (Encapsulated Post Script) and TIFF (Tagged Image) file formats. EPS files have the advantage of scalability, while TIFFs can be opened by a broader range of software. Patterns on the CD are numbered to match the page number in the book.

Whichever type of computer you use, you'll see a folder of EPS files, and a folder of TIFFs to use in case your software is unable to take advantage of EPS.

To use the files, simply pop the disk into your computer's CD drive, and a window will appear with two folders. Between the two file types offered, you'll be able to use these images in a huge range of common applications, including Adobe Photoshop, Adobe Photoshop Elements, Adobe Illustrator, Macromedia Freehand and even Microsoft Word. Choose your software to fit your project.

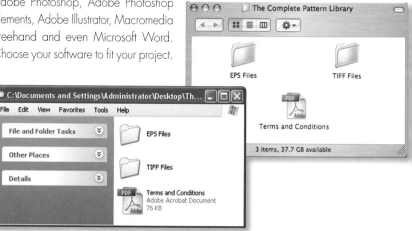

Using this book

The patterns in this book are numbered on the disk to match their page number in this book, and saved in both EPS and TIFF formats. Choosing your pattern is simplicity itself:

1 Browse through this book – the patterns begin on page 12 – and select the pattern of your choice. Each pattern also has three suggested colourways described in terms of CMYK – Cyan, Magenta, Yellow and Black (Key).

2 Insert the CD into your computer's CD-ROM drive and open the folder. Depending on whether you want to work with EPS files or TIFF files, select the appropriately named folder.

3 If you'd like more detailed instructions on using your pattern, follow the steps on pages 6–7 (for bitmap software) or pages 8–9 (for vector software). These steps show you how to apply colour to your pattern, and to repeat it across an infinite space.

4 You're now free to use the pattern however you like; we've made a few suggestions on pages 10–11 but the limits of your imagination are really all that's stopping you.

5 You're free to distribute artwork you've created using the patterns, according to the terms and conditions on the CD.

File formats: EPS vs TIFF

Computers interpret images in two radically different ways, as bitmapped grids of small squares – pixels – or as mathematical descriptions of shapes called vector graphics. Bitmapped images, of which TIFF is a common type, can be opened by almost any software that reads images. Vector graphics, since they describe shapes, are better suited to patterns because you can scale them infinitely without loss of quality. In order of preference, it's best to use a vector-based program (like Adobe Illustrator or Macromedia Freehand); a bitmap program that can load vector files (like Photoshop); or, failing either, any other graphics program, in which case use the TIFF files.

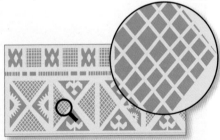

Vector (EPS)

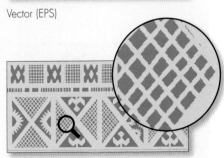

Bitmapped (TIFF)

Working with an image editor

Here is one way to create patterns using the CD and Adobe Photoshop Elements. Applications like this work on pixels – tiny squares that, when viewed together, appear to form an image. For this reason, resolution (the level of detail) is important. If it is too low, the individual pixels will be visible. Before you start, you'll need to know how wide you'd like each recurrence of the pattern to be.

1 Using *File > New* from the menu, create a new, blank image the size you'd like to cover with your pattern. In this example, it's a 15- x 10-cm (6- x 4-inch) postcard at a resolution of 300 pixels per inch (ppi).

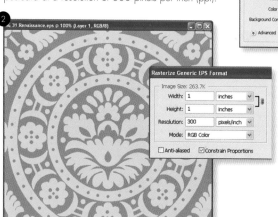

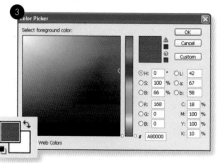

2 Insert the CD and open one of the pattern files. If possible, you should use an EPS file. Set the size you'd like each repeat to be, set the resolution to match the setting in step 1, make sure the Anti-aliased option is off and then click OK. Your chosen pattern will appear without any colour added.

3 To replace one of the grey shades with a colour of your choice, first click on the foreground colour on the Tools bar and set it to the colour you want using the Colour Picker.

4 Now select the Paint Bucket tool, and, on the Tool Options bar, turn off the Contiguous option. When you click on one area in the pattern, all areas of that colour are replaced with your new colour

5 Change the foreground colour on the Tools bar and, as necessary, repeat steps 3 and 4 for all the shades of grey in the pattern.

6 Select the whole pattern using *Image > Select All,* then click on *Edit > Define Pattern from Selection…* Give your pattern a name you will understand, since it will be available to you from now on.

7 Switch to your target image – in this case the postcard we made in step 1 – then click on the Paint Bucket tool. Select Pattern under the Fill option and then click the Pattern button – you will be able to select your newly defined pattern.

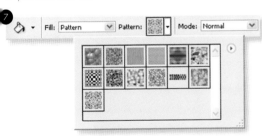

8 Click within the image to apply your pattern to the whole page. (If you first select an area or define a shape, the Paint Bucket will only fill that area or shape with the pattern.)

Working with an illustration package

Illustration software, or 'vector-graphics' programs, work by defining shapes mathematically, in terms of their points, lines and curves. Since the image is not composed of pixels, the shapes can be scaled up or down to any level without loss of detail. All that's necessary is to add colour and repeat the pattern as many times as you need.

1 Open your chosen pattern as an EPS file in your graphics program. We're using Adobe Illustrator CS, but similar tools are available in other versions or alternative software.

2 Use the *File > Document Setup...* option to define the final size of the page you would like your pattern to appear on. You can choose from the list, or select Custom and add your own Width and Height.

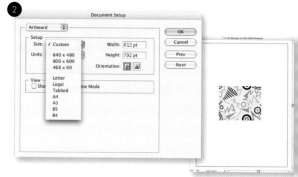

3 Your pattern will now appear in the centre of the page. Now we need to add colour to it. Open the Layers palette (*Window > Layers*) and select a layer that you want to alter by clicking on the round 'target' icon to the right of the layer name.

4 All the objects on that layer of the pattern will be highlighted.

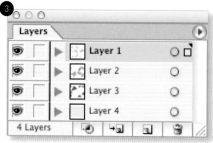

5 Use the Swatch palette to add colour. Either open a Swatch Library or create a new colour by clicking New Swatch using the palette menu (circular icon, top right of the palette). We will click on New Swatch to create a new colour.

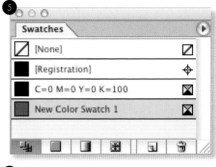

6 Using the colour picker, define a new colour for this part of the pattern.

7 Repeat steps 3 to 6 for each layer you'd like to add a new colour to. (Note that more advanced users can alter the colour or shape of individual elements within the pattern.)

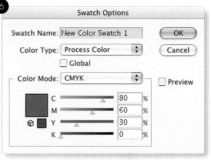

8 Select all the layers using the menu option *Select > All*, then group them using *Object > Group*. Move the pattern to the top left corner of your page. Select the Move tool, and click and drag the pattern.

9 Enable Smart Guides using the View menu, then carefully move the cursor to any point along the left-hand edge of your pattern. The word *path* will appear.

10 Hold down the Alt (Option) key and drag the pointer to the right (or along the direction you wish to repeat your pattern). Try to keep roughly to the automatic guide. As you reach the other side of the pattern, the word *intersect* will appear, and you can release the mouse button. A copy of the pattern will appear in exact alignment.

11 Simply repeat this process as many times as you need. Anything that appears outside the printing area will not be printed.

Pattern creativity

There are literally thousands of uses for a pattern that tessellates, like all those in this book, in a grid of rectangles. These infinitely expandable images can become anything from gift-wrap to wallpaper for a doll's house. Here are a few ideas.

Picture frame

It's possible to create a personalized frame effect by picking colours from, or colours that complement, your picture. Using any image editor, create a page larger than your final picture and copy your pattern as on page 7. Delete an area in the center of your pattern and then place your image in a layer beneath it. Either select the colours of your choice, or use the Eyedropper tool to select your colour scheme. That way, you're using colours from the image itself.

The shadow effect adds a solid feel to the frame.

Website

HyperText Markup Language (HTML), the computer code that describes Web pages, has a standard option to include a background image that – if it isn't large enough to fill the page – will automatically tessellate for you. All Web page software will allow you access to the 'background' function, or you can simply alter the text itself.

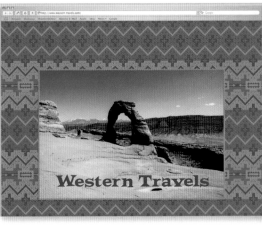

Use the patterns to personalize your website.

Open your chosen pattern in an image editor, apply your chosen colour scheme, but don't make it a repeating pattern. Instead, choose the Save for Web... option and save the file as a .GIF file. In the Web page, add the code <body background='[your filename]'> and your image will be automatically tiled.

Desktop wallpaper

Open your image in an image-editing program and save it as a .BMP file, and you can use it as your desktop backdrop (or 'wallpaper'). Simply right-click (Ctrl-click on a Mac) and click browse. Select Tile from the options, and your pattern can sit behind your work.

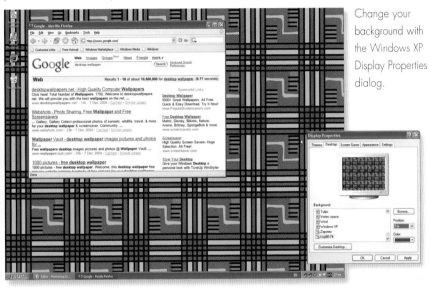

Change your background with the Windows XP Display Properties dialog.

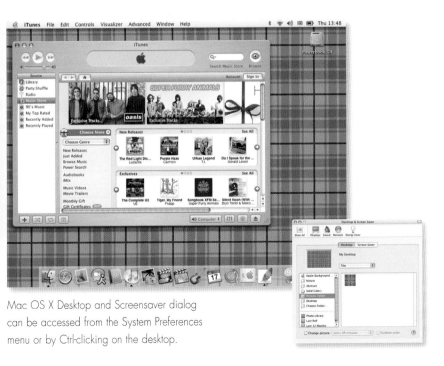

Mac OS X Desktop and Screensaver dialog can be accessed from the System Preferences menu or by Ctrl-clicking on the desktop.

11

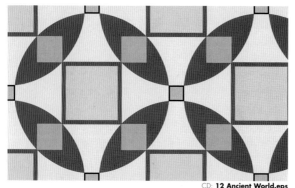

Ancient World
Greece, c.AD 500

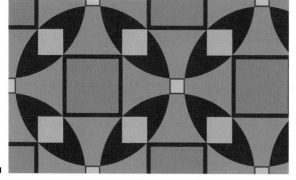

CD: **12 Ancient World.eps**

A tile pattern unearthed during excavations at Eleusis, this design borrows from the strict geometric format developed by the Ancient Egyptians. The crisp, harmonious blues on the original are punctuated with the contrasting smaller squares, while the arrangement of shapes lends a certain tightness to the composition. Allowing the large squares to dominate will produce a star-like effect on this surprisingly adaptable pattern.

1
Layer 1 25c 25m 25y 5k
Layer 2 60c 80m 35y 30k
Layer 3 30c 10m 70y 0k
Layer 4 60c 90m 35y 30k
Layer 5 80c 15m 40y 5k
Layer 6 70c 30m 5y 0k

2
Layer 1 0c 30m 80y 0k
Layer 2 70c 60m 90y 0k
Layer 3 0c 30m 80y 0k
Layer 4 70c 60m 90y 0k
Layer 5 0c 70m 90y 0k
Layer 6 20c 20m 20y 10k

3
Layer 1 60c 90m 90y 0k
Layer 2 90c 70m 40y 0k
Layer 3 30c 45m 45y 0k
Layer 4 90c 70m 40y 0k
Layer 5 60c 80m 40y 0k
Layer 6 30c 40m 40y 0k

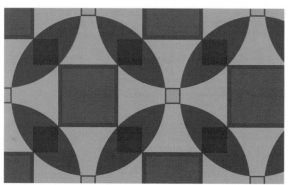

1

2

3

Romano-Byzantine

Italy, c.AD 700

This design is based on marble pavement fragments found in the basilica of Rome's Santa Maria in Cosmedin and is typical of floor decoration in the time of Pope Hadrian I. The simple triangular forms lend themselves to a variety of art and craft applications, and experimentation with scale and colour may render the pattern strikingly modern.

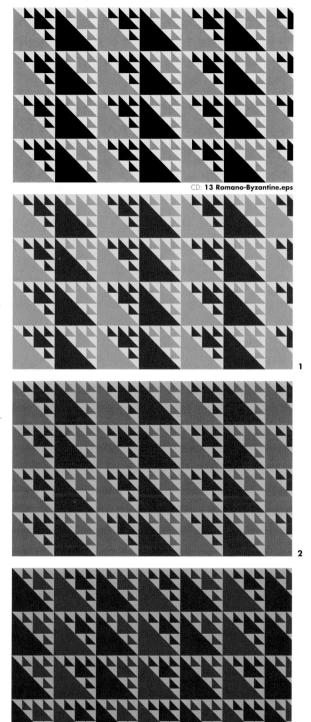

CD: **13 Romano-Byzantine.eps**

1

1
Layer 1   80c 90m 80y 20k
Layer 2   50c 30m 60y 0k
Layer 3   10c 10m 30y 0k

2
Layer 1   15c 100m 100y 5k
Layer 2   15c 80m 100y 5k
Layer 3   0c 45m 90y 0k

3
Layer 1   90c 65m 50y 35k
Layer 2   70c 80m 60y 55k
Layer 3   25c 30m 45y 5k

2

3

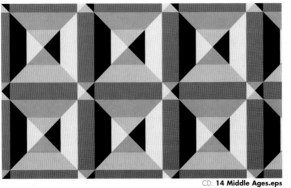

Middle Ages
Italy, c.1000

CD: **14 Middle Ages.eps**

A marble pavement mosaic from Saint Mark's cathedral in Venice, this pattern features the colour combination of red, ochre and black that was common during this period. In a manner reminiscent of marquetry, each repeat is based on the division of five bands of equal width, which also gives the whole pattern a robust aspect. Pyramids emerge or the squares on the diagonal 'hover' via the deployment of different colourways.

1
Layer 1   30c 20m 40y 0k
Layer 2   30c 70m 90y 0k
Layer 3   60c 80m 60y 60k
Layer 4   30c 40m 90y 0k
Layer 5   5c 10m 40y 0k

2
Layer 1   0c 0m 0y 50k
Layer 2   60c 30m 10y 10k
Layer 3   60c 40m 30y 10k
Layer 4   30c 30m 30y 10k
Layer 5   10c10m 20y 10k

3
Layer 1   70c 30m 20y 0k
Layer 2   50c 40m 40y 0k
Layer 3   50c 50m 50y 100k
Layer 4   70c 100m 100y 0k
Layer 5   25c 20m 20y 0k

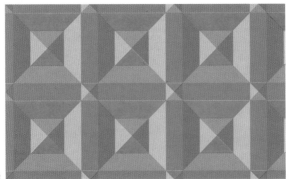

1

2

3

Romano-Byzantine

Italy, c.1100

The trellis-like effect of this enamelled mosaic pattern from the Palatine Chapel in Palermo can be emphasized by increasing the contrast between the green diagonal stripes and the elements coloured red in the original design. For a very different effect, selecting close tints of cool blues will deliver a design that is both mannered and easy on the eye.

CD: **15 Romano-Byzantine.eps**

1

1
Layer 1   10c 30m 60y 0k
Layer 2   0c 10m 40y 0k
Layer 3   0c 70m 70y 0k
Layer 4   40c 20m 60y 0k

2
Layer 1   70c 0m 40y 0k
Layer 2   60c 100m 0y 30k
Layer 3   100c 70m 0y 0k
Layer 4   0c 80m 0y 0k

3
Layer 1   70c 60m 90y 0k
Layer 2   90c 70m 0y 0k
Layer 3   0c 70m 90y 0k
Layer 4   70c 100m 90y 0k

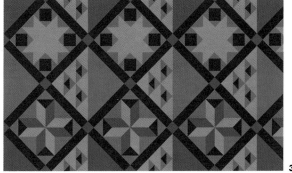

2

3

Arabian

c.1200

The ingenuity of this deceptively simple device may be without contextual equal. Precise draftsmanship and a mathematically exacting correlation between line volume and length create the positive and negative space that yields the repeating symbol. It represents fertility, although a snowflake or a waterwheel may also be seen. A monochromatic palette will make the design feel less rigid and more textural.

1
Layer 1   100c 20m 30y 0k
Layer 2   60c 20m 10y 0k
Layer 3   50c 100m 30y 0k

2
Layer 1   100c 60m 0y 0k
Layer 2   0c 10m 100y 0k
Layer 3   90c 0m 10y 0k

3
Layer 1   60c 90m 0y 0k
Layer 2   0c 40m 100y 0k
Layer 3   0c 80m 100y 0k

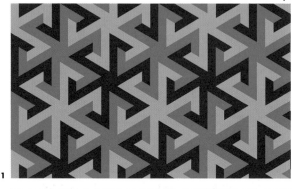

1

2

3

Arabian-Moorish

Cairo, c.1250

This floor and wainscot mosaic pattern was made from coloured marble inlaid with stucco. The design, which radiates from an eight-pointed star, creating all sorts of irregular shapes before the repeat is resolved, marks a move away from the stricter geometric conventions observed in earlier Islamic pattern work. Replacing the original design's earthy tones with brighter colours imparts a fresher look.

1
Layer 1   90c 20m 40y 0k
Layer 2   60c 40m 50y 0k
Layer 3   10c 50m 70y 0k
Layer 4   0c 10m 40y 0k
Layer 5   30c 70m 60y 0k

2
Layer 1   50c 50m 50y 100k
Layer 2   30c 100m 0y 0k
Layer 3   0c 50m 100y 0k
Layer 4   0c 90m 10y 0k
Layer 5   90c 90m 0y 0k

3
Layer 1   70c 30m 30y 0k
Layer 2   50c 40m 40y 0k
Layer 3   50c 20m 40y 0k
Layer 4   0c 10m 40y 0k
Layer 5   30c 50m 70y 0k

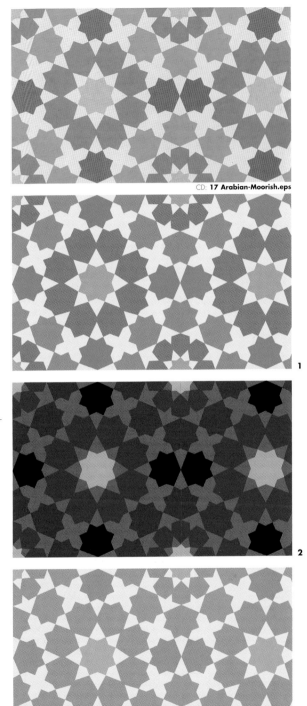

CD: **17 Arabian-Moorish.eps**

1

2

3

Islamic
c.1250

CD: **18 Islamic.eps**

This thirteenth-century mosaic design is a more complex development of a classic Islamic pattern format, simpler versions of which can be traced back to AD 500. Through the precise, balanced distribution of line work, twelve- and eight-pointed stars combine with other geometric shapes for an elaborate effect. The rich colours of the original are typical, but a less contrasting palette would add to the textural effect.

1

Layer 1	0c 15m 55y 10k
Layer 2	5c 60m 70y 5k
Layer 3	20c 0m 30y 35k
Layer 4	10c 0m 15y 5k

2

Layer 1	55c 0m 10y 0k
Layer 2	50c 55m 0y 10k
Layer 3	60c 20m 10y 30k
Layer 4	10c 0m 0y 10k

3

Layer 1	15c 35m 45y 15k
Layer 2	0c 0m 0y 85k
Layer 3	20c 20m 30y 10k
Layer 4	5c 5m 10y 5k

1

2

3

Islamic

Cairo, c.1300

The six-pointed star is the primary building block of Islamic decorative art, yielding a hexagon and an equilateral triangle through its repeat and subdivision. It is the interplay between these geometric forms and the interlacing of their outline shapes that give character to this ancient pattern format, which has been inventively exploited by successive generations in the creation of tiles and mosaics.

CD: **19 Islamic.eps**

1

1
Layer 1   0c 15m 0y 15k
Layer 2   80c 80m 30y 80k
Layer 3   0c 0m 50y 0k
Layer 4   0c 20m 35y 0k
Layer 5   0c 15m 0y 15k

2
Layer 1   0c 100m 35y 0k
Layer 2   70c 70m 70y 70k
Layer 3   0c 0m 100y 0k
Layer 4   0c 100m 30y 0k
Layer 5   100c 15m 0y 15k

3
Layer 1   0c 20m 100y 0k
Layer 2   0c 0m 0y 100k
Layer 3   100c 0m 50y 0k
Layer 4   0c 20m 100y 0k
Layer 5   0c 100m 0y 0k

2

3

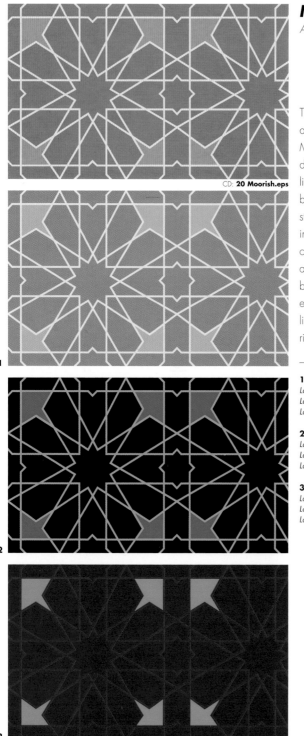

CD: **20 Moorish.eps**

Moorish

Algeria, c.1300

The walls surrounding the ancient Algerian town of Mansourah were once decorated with this bold linear pattern, which is based on a twelve-pointed star – a familiar feature in Moorish design. The celestial associations here are clear, and a dark blue or indigo ground, for example, will lift the paler line work to produce a rich nocturnal effect.

1
Layer 1   0c 10m 40y 0k
Layer 2   50c 10m 40y 0k
Layer 3   50c 50m 50y 0k

2
Layer 1   0c 50m 100y 0k
Layer 2   100c 50m 0y 0k
Layer 3   50c 0m 0y 100k

3
Layer 1   0c 100m 10y 0k
Layer 2   100c 0m 20y 0k
Layer 3   100c 100m 0y 0k

Renaissance

Italy, c.1450

In fifteenth-century Italy, it became the fashion to borrow design styles from other cultures and traditions. Such is the case with this wall hanging, which is clearly inspired by earlier Oriental work. The balance between the volumes of line work and ground achieves a feeling of opulence while leaving the whole tastefully uncluttered and tranquil.

CD: **21 Renaissance.eps**

1

1

Layer 1	0c 10m 30y 0k
Layer 2	30c 70m 80y 0k
Layer 3	30c 30m 40y 0k
Layer 4	80c 100m 80y 0k

2

Layer 1	0c 50m 100y 0k
Layer 2	100c 0m 20y 0k
Layer 3	40c 100m 90y 0k
Layer 4	100c 80m 50y 0k

3

Layer 1	10c 10m 30y 0k
Layer 2	80c 70m 80y 10k
Layer 3	20c 40m 70y 0k
Layer 4	50c 80m 80y 0k

2

3

CD: **22 Art Deco.eps**

1

Art Deco
France, c.1890

Row upon row of empty
chambers, or endless
squares of chocolate?
Whatever one sees here,
this design from a Parisian
tile-pattern catalogue
certainly draws us in,
teasing with its optical
trickery. The graphic thrust
of the Art Deco movement
was founded on simple
illusionistic devices such
as this pattern, and
experimenting with colour
and orientation may yield
more unexpected forms.

1
Layer 1   0c 10m 40y 0k
Layer 2   20c 20m 40y 0k
Layer 3   60c 60m 70y 0k

2
Layer 1   0c 30m 100y 0k
Layer 2   100c 0m 50y 0k
Layer 3   70c 100m 0y 0k

3
Layer 1   30c 40m 50y 0k
Layer 2   50c 100m 90y 10k
Layer 3   70c 80m 70y 30k

2

3

Art Deco

France, 1925

The celebrated Parisian *Exposition des Arts Décoratifs* in 1925 was the designers' showpiece of all things iconoclastic and avant-garde in the interwar years, and it effectively gave its name to the Art Deco movement. The simple rectilinear shapes seen in this pattern are typical of the approach, which marked a move away from the more directly representational renderings of the Art Nouveau school.

CD: **23 Art Deco.eps**

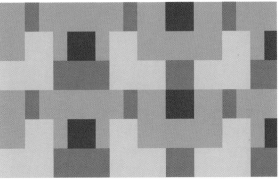

1

1
Layer 1   40c 0m 50y 0k
Layer 2   60c 60m 20y 0k
Layer 3   90c 70m 40y 0k
Layer 4   60c 20m 20y 0k

2
Layer 1   0c 70m 90y 0k
Layer 2   100c 90m 50y 0k
Layer 3   100c 90m 0y 0k
Layer 4   20c 40m 50y 0k

3
Layer 1   0c 10m 40y 0k
Layer 2   30c 50m 70y 0k
Layer 3   70c 30m 30y 0k
Layer 4   50c 40m 40y 0k

2

3

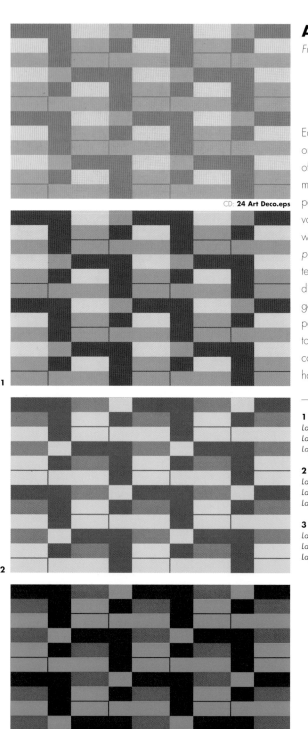

CD: **24 Art Deco.eps**

1

2

3

Art Deco
France, 1930

Edouard Benedictus was one of the leading lights of the French Art Deco movement, and this classic pattern from his *Relais* volume of printed designs was produced using the *pochoir* stencil colouring technique. The ordered divisions and precise geometric proportions use positive and negative space to achieve a tight, balanced composition, and the whole has a real sense of urgency.

1
Layer 1   80c 20m 5y 70k
Layer 2   50c 0m 5y 0k
Layer 3   80c 20m 5y 0k

2
Layer 1   70c 80m 90y 0k
Layer 2   20c 70m 90y 0k
Layer 3   0c 20m 90y 0k

3
Layer 1   90c 100m 0y 0k
Layer 2   0c 90m 10y 0k
Layer 3   100c 0m 40y 0k

Talish

Azerbaijan, Traditional

The Muslim Talish, who reside on the Caspian coast, are well known for their production of rich, colourful handicrafts and are highly respected for their traditional trades such as rug-making. The physical limitations of the loom determine the simplicity of this pattern, whose warm, vibrant colours complete a design typical of the region.

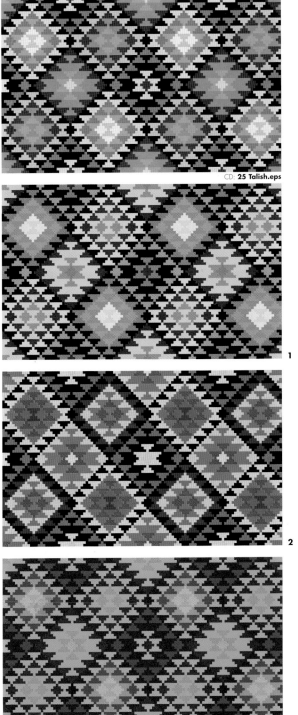

CD: **25 Talish.eps**

1

1

Layer 1	0c 60m 90y 0k
Layer 2	50c 50m 50y 100k
Layer 3	0c 100m 50y 0k
Layer 4	0c 30m 90y 0k
Layer 5	40c 60m 0y 0k
Layer 6	40c 60m 90y 0k
Layer 7	0c 20m 90y 0k
Layer 8	10c 10m 20y 0k

2

Layer 1	90c 20m 40y 20k
Layer 2	0c 0m 0y 100k
Layer 3	0c 0m 30y 20k
Layer 4	100c 5m 30y 20k
Layer 5	0c 90m 90y 0k
Layer 6	0c 0m 0y 20k
Layer 7	100c 10m 0y 70k
Layer 8	90c 0m 0y 50k

3

Layer 1	80c 80m 80y 0k
Layer 2	100c 100m 0y 0k
Layer 3	0c 100m 100y 0k
Layer 4	80c 0m 40y 0k
Layer 5	70c 30m 0y 0k
Layer 6	70c 50m 90y 0k
Layer 7	50c 30m 20y 0k
Layer 8	30c 30m 30y 0k

2

3

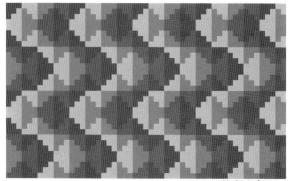

CD: **26 Andean.eps**

Andean
Peru, Traditional

Textiles were used as a form of currency in ancient Peru, in a system whereby finer detailing or the use of more vibrant or elusive colours would accord more value to a particular item. Of all the traditional Peruvian weave patterns, this is one of the more instantly recognizable, and the ancient design can still be found on handicrafts produced today.

1
Layer 1   10c 10m 100y 0k
Layer 2   50c 50m 10y 0k
Layer 3   40c 30m 100y 0k
Layer 4   80c 90m 10y 0k

2
Layer 1   30c 40m 40y 0k
Layer 2   60c 90m 90y 0k
Layer 3   50c 60m 60y 0k
Layer 4   80c 80m 10y 50k

3
Layer 1   20c 20m 30y 0k
Layer 2   90c 0m 20y 0k
Layer 3   50c 50m 50y 100k
Layer 4   100c 60m 0y 0k

1

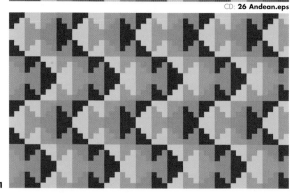

2

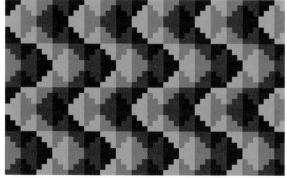

3

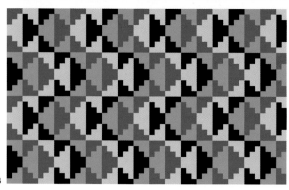

Op Art

Britain, 2004

The Op Art movement brought an abstract, mathematically oriented aesthetic to 1960s art. Using simple repeating forms and colours, these artists' works were full of moiré effects, illusions of exaggerated depth, tonal vibrations and other visual tricks and deceptions. The shimmering disks in this pattern follow that model.

1
Layer 1   100c 20m 0y 0k
Layer 2   0c 100m 100y 0k
Layer 3   0c 0m 0y 70k

2
Layer 1   100c 0m 50y 0k
Layer 2   80c 100m 0y 0k
Layer 3   90c 80m 0y 0k

3
Layer 1   0c 100m 100y 0k
Layer 2   30c 100m 0y 0k
Layer 3   60c 80m 60y 60k

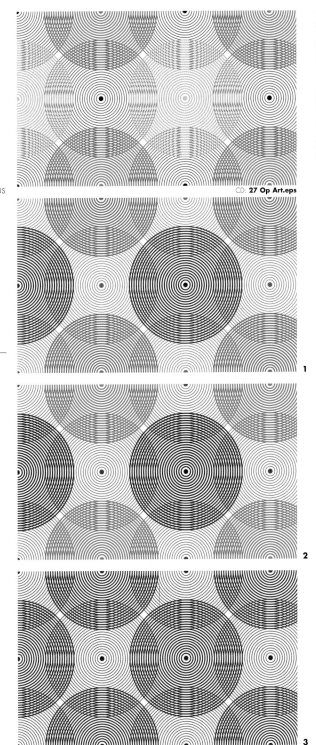

CD: **27 Op Art.eps**

CD: **28 Asian.eps**

Asian
India, Traditional

Some of the guiding principles of traditional Indian design may be observed in this printed fabric, including the sensitive treatment of natural forms, the formal yet unstuffy composition and the absence of unnecessary ornament. On the original, the leaves running through the diagonal were printed in gold, which settles handsomely on any dark ground such as an inky blue or a chocolate brown.

1

1
Layer 1   20c 20m 30y 0k
Layer 2   0c 100m 100y 0k
Layer 3   40c 30m 60y 0k
Layer 4   70c 90m 100y 0k

2

2
Layer 1   30c 20m 30y 0k
Layer 2   70c 30m 10y 0k
Layer 3   0c 60m 10y 0k
Layer 4   80c 50m 10y 0k

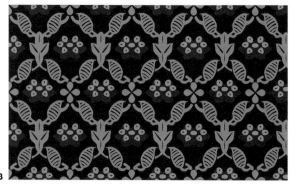

3

3
Layer 1   30c 50m 90y 0k
Layer 2   100c 90m 0y 0k
Layer 3   0c 70m 90y 0k
Layer 4   80c 100m 0y 0k

Oriental
Japan, Traditional

Japanese designers have seen their more linear work printed onto the world's finest silks and satins for centuries, and craftspeople in this field are still held in the highest regard. This bold robe design uses a leaf motif within a dissected circular shape suggestive of the moon. Contrasting light and dark greens will produce a lush vegetative effect.

CD: **29 Oriental.eps**

1

1
Layer 1   60c 0m 20y 100k
Layer 2   60c 0m 20y 100k
Layer 3   60c 0m 20y 0k

2
Layer 1   0c 80m 100y 0k
Layer 2   90c 0m 20y 0k
Layer 3   100c 60m 0y 0k

3
Layer 1   90c 100m 0y 0k
Layer 2   100c 30m 0y 0k
Layer 3   0c 90m 10y 0k

2

3

CD: **30 Asian.eps**

Asian
India, c.1400

The aster plant was regarded as sacred by the Indian followers of the Iranian prophet Zoroaster, after whom it was named. From the thirteenth to the fifteenth centuries, the motif was widely used for tapestries and clothes, and it also decorated everyday tools and household utensils. Aster patterns were typically woven, embroidered or printed in red, green and yellow or gold.

1

1
Layer 1   70c 40m 60y 0k
Layer 2   0c 80m 100y 0k
Layer 3   0c 10m 40y 0k

2
Layer 1   90c 100m 20y 0k
Layer 2   50c 100m 90y 0k
Layer 3   50c 40m 40y 0k

3
Layer 1   100c 70m 0y 0k
Layer 2   70c 100m 0y 0k
Layer 3   0c 50m 0y 0k

2

3

Renaissance

Spain, c.1500

Patterns such as this one were manufactured in fine materials such as silk damask for robes of high clerical office. This design bears elements of the Moorish work of the previous two centuries, modified by a tendency toward the gentler shapes that were popular during the Renaissance. The combination of monochromatic palette and formal composition in this example can be compared to much Victorian pattern design.

1
Layer 1 70c 30m 70y 0k
Layer 2 40c 10m 50y 0k

2
Layer 1 70c 100m 0y 0k
Layer 2 0c 30m 100y 0k

3
Layer 1 60c 100m 30y 0k
Layer 2 10c 20m 20y 40k

CD: **31 Renaissance.eps**

1

2

3

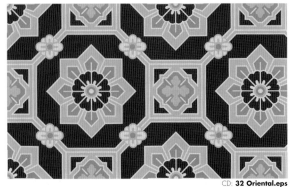

Oriental
Japan, c.1600

CD: **32 Oriental.eps**

This woven fabric pattern teams floral motifs with squares and precise line work in a typically formal arrangement. Fabric samples of different styles and colours were often brought together and used by the Japanese to decorate their screens in a patchwork fashion. The green and brown from the original design can be substituted with brighter colours for an upbeat yet mannered composition.

1

2

1
Layer 1	20c 10m 30y 0k
Layer 2	80c 30m 30y 0k
Layer 3	30c 50m 80y 0k
Layer 4	90c 60m 60y 0k

2
Layer 1	70c 90m 20y 0k
Layer 2	90c 0m 20y 0k
Layer 3	0c 20m 80y 0k
Layer 4	0c 90m 30y 0k

3
Layer 1	30c 40m 40y 0k
Layer 2	60c 70m 40y 0k
Layer 3	60c 50m 30y 0k
Layer 4	70c 90m 50y 10k

3

Chinoiserie

France, c.1600

Seafaring advances increased trade possibilities between Europe and the East at this time, and a vogue began for silks imported from China and elsewhere. European manufacturers soon found themselves producing imitations of Chinese wares, and this example couples gold with a rich red for a luxurious effect. Such rhythmic floral patterns may have influenced the work of the Arts and Crafts movement some 300 years later.

1
Layer 1   0c 40m 50y 0k
Layer 2   30c 20m 50y 0k
Layer 3   10c 80m 50y 0k

2
Layer 1   70c 100m 0y 0k
Layer 2   100c 0m 50y 0k
Layer 3   0c 30m 100y 0k

3
Layer 1   10c 20m 20y 40k
Layer 2   10c 100m 60y 0k
Layer 3   70c 70m 70y 50k

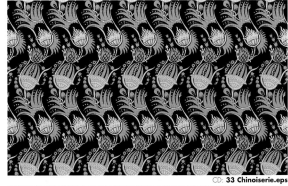

CD: **33 Chinoiserie.eps**

1

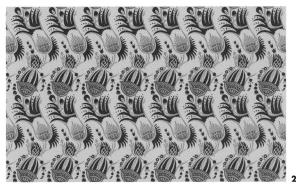

2

3

Victorian
Britain, c.1850

This pattern was originally created for a wallpaper and is from a time when, through growing design awareness, more affluent British households were experiencing a decorating fixation. The rounded flower heads are set off elegantly against the spiky rendering of the leaves, and each repeat has just enough space around it to leave the pattern dynamic yet unfussy.

1

1
Layer 1	0c 10m 30y 0k
Layer 2	0c 0m 0y 0k
Layer 3	30c 60m 90y 10k

2
Layer 1	60c 30m 40y 0k
Layer 2	90c 50m 40y 0k
Layer 3	30c 20m 20y 0k

3
Layer 1	70c 70m 90y 0k
Layer 2	0c 10m 90y 0k
Layer 3	90c 100m 0y 0k

2

3

Victorian

Britain, c.1850

CD: **35 Victorian.eps**

This is an exemplar of the more subtle and controlled side of Victorian design. Each motif is cleverly linked to its neighbours by the graceful vine device, and the flat, earthy colours of the original serve to sustain the understatement and restraint. The pattern will, however, work equally well with more contrasting colour selections.

1

1
Layer 1   20c 40m 50y 0k
Layer 2   50c 70m 50y 0k

2
Layer 1   70c 60m 30y 50k
Layer 2   0c 50m 10y 0k

3
Layer 1   20c 50m 80y 0k
Layer 2   80c 50m 40y 0k

2

3

Arts and Crafts
Britain, 1883

William Morris strove to enrich people's lives through artistry prompted by nature. This hand-printed pattern is among the more graphic of Morris & Co.'s wallpaper designs, and it has a formal yet rhythmic composition that is rendered flat by the stencil-like effect. The muted greyish-greens and ochre of the original may be brought closer together in hue for a more textural, even flatter, effect.

CD: **36 Arts and Crafts.eps**

1

2

3

1
Layer 1   20c 10m 40y 0k
Layer 2   10c 40m 50y 0k
Layer 3   70c 30m 50y 0k
Layer 4   5c 5m 20y 0k

2
Layer 1   0c 60m 40y 0k
Layer 2   20c 50m 70y 0k
Layer 3   40c 90m 0y 0k
Layer 4   100c 80m 50y 0k

3
Layer 1   90c 0m 10y 0k
Layer 2   50c 0m 100y 0k
Layer 3   90c 40m 0y 0k
Layer 4   0c 20m 90y 0k

Art Nouveau

France, c.1890

The Art Nouveau style was characterized by the exploration of nature's rhythms through expressive representations of closely observed subjects. Highly stylized patterns (this one was mass-produced for a fabric), such as irises over rippling water, were commonly rendered in a muted palette tending toward sage greens and greyish-blues, but this pattern can be given an air of modernity with the use of more luminous colours.

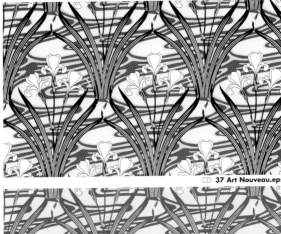

CD: **37 Art Nouveau.eps**

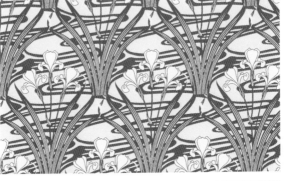

1

1

Layer 1	0c 0m 60y 0k
Layer 2	50c 70m 80y 20k
Layer 3	50c 70m 80y 20k
Layer 4	0c 0m 40y 0k
Layer 5	0c 80m 65y 25k
Layer 6	0c 0m 70y 15k
Layer 7	0c 5m 5y 5k
Layer 8	5c 0m 45y 0k

2

2

Layer 1	0c 20m 70y 0k
Layer 2	50c 70m 80y 20k
Layer 3	50c 0m 80y 40k
Layer 4	100c 0m 20y 0k
Layer 5	0c 70m 0y 25k
Layer 6	0c 20m 20y 15k
Layer 7	0c 0m 5y 10k
Layer 8	0c 40m 60y 0k

3

Layer 1	15c 5m 60y 0k
Layer 2	0c 10m 100y 0k
Layer 3	50c 0m 85y 25k
Layer 4	0c 50m 0y 0k
Layer 5	100c 0m 0y 0k
Layer 6	0c 100m 0y 0k
Layer 7	5c 5m 0y 5k
Layer 8	15c 5m 60y 0k

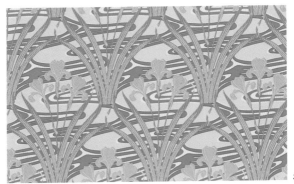

3

CD: **38 Art Nouveau.eps**

1

2

3

Art Nouveau
France, c.1890

Reminiscent of stained-glass work, this pattern derives from a decorative stencil pattern originally created by M P Verneuil – one of the pivotal figures in the development of the Art Nouveau style and philosophy. The artist's work here exemplifies the movement's tendency toward sensitive flowing shapes, underpinned by a strong affinity with the natural world. The black outlines will support the most adventurous of colour combinations.

1
Layer 1   20c 20m 70y 0k
Layer 2   10c 20m 80y 25k
Layer 3   40c 50m 90y 20k
Layer 4   80c 80m 80y 50k
Layer 5   60c 15m 60y 15k
Layer 6   55c 0m 45y 15k
Layer 7   10c 0m 70y 0k
Layer 8   40c 0m 60y 10k

2
Layer 1   15c 40m 70y 15k
Layer 2   0c 35m 75y 0k
Layer 3   40c 50m 90y 20k
Layer 4   65c 65m 80y 55k
Layer 5   15c 50m 35y 15k
Layer 6   30c 25m 0y 15k
Layer 7   20c 30m 60y 0k
Layer 8   5c 20m 70y 0k

3
Layer 1   15c 40m 0y 10k
Layer 2   50c 0m 0y 0k
Layer 3   70c 65m 0y 20k
Layer 4   45c 45m 45y 80k
Layer 5   80c 25m 40y 30k
Layer 6   65c 0m 45y 15k
Layer 7   30c 15m 50y 0k
Layer 8   20c 10m 85y 0k

European
France, 1911

A design for pavements from a French tile catalogue forms the basis of this pattern. Various influences from the history of decorative art are at work here, including the time-honoured use of the hexagon as both the building block and the overlapping and interlocking feature that binds the floral shapes. The earthy colours, too, call to mind more ancient work.

CD: **39 European.eps**

1
Layer 1 0c 60m 50y 0k
Layer 2 0c 10m 30y 0k
Layer 3 90c 70m 50y 0k
Layer 4 0c 5m 15y 0k

2
Layer 1 70c 30m 20y 0k
Layer 2 50c 40m 0y 50k
Layer 3 50c 50m 50y 100k
Layer 4 40c 50m 20y 0k

3
Layer 1 30c 100m 0y 0k
Layer 2 0c 90m 10y 0k
Layer 3 90c 90m 0y 0k
Layer 4 0c 0m 0y 0k

CD: **40 Oriental.eps**

Oriental
China, c.1400

The wavy organic forms lend
an almost marine quality to
this fabric design, with its
dominant black and aquatic
blue. The repeat has at its
heart a form that may be
seen as what we call a
paisley motif: the ancient
and mysterious symbol that
appears time and again
throughout the history of
symbolic art. Allowing
the details to recede will
give the black areas an
impression of fretwork.

1

1
Layer 1   100c 0m 0y 70k
Layer 2   10c 0m 0y 20k
Layer 3   70c 20m 0y 20k

2
Layer 1   0c 20m 100y 0k
Layer 2   30c 100m 0y 0k
Layer 3   90c 100m 0y 0k

3
Layer 1   40c 70m 50y 0k
Layer 2   0c 10m 40y 0k
Layer 3   50c 0m 30y 0k

2

3

Oriental

China, c.1600–1800

Chinese work at its elegant best can be found on this pattern from a painted china bottle. The method of linking the floral forms with a unifying line is known as the continuous-stem principle, and it adds a delicate flowing grace to the composition. The black of the leaves and stems here may be replaced with green for a more verdant feel.

CD: **41 Oriental.eps**

1

Layer 1	30c 0m 0y 50k
Layer 2	80c 10m 50y 0k
Layer 3	100c 20m 70y 0k
Layer 4	0c 0m 0y 100k
Layer 5	0c 0m 0y 0k
Layer 6	0c 100m 100y 0k
Layer 7	0c 10m 40y 0k

2

Layer 1	60c 30m 40y 0k
Layer 2	30c 30m 10y 0k
Layer 3	90c 50m 40y 0k
Layer 4	90c 50m 40y 0k
Layer 5	30c 30m 10y 0k
Layer 6	70c 80m 20y 0k
Layer 7	30c 20m 20y 0k

3

Layer 1	0c 20m 100y 0k
Layer 2	0c 20m 100y 0k
Layer 3	0c 0m 0y 100k
Layer 4	0c 0m 0y 100k
Layer 5	0c 0m 0y 0k
Layer 6	0c 100m 50y 0k
Layer 7	30c 0m 100y 0k

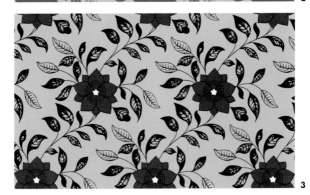

CD: **42 Oriental.eps**

Oriental
Japan, c.1800

The abiding Japanese theme of nature's cycles is apparent in this fabric design, which derives from the long-established Kano school. Autumn reds and browns will invest the foliage with an aspect suggestive of that season. Alternatively, dark-green leaves against a pale ground with contrasting deep reds for the berries may give the pattern a wintry feel.

1

1
Layer 1   10c 20m 20y 40k
Layer 2   70c 80m 30y 50k

2
Layer 1   0c 30m 100y 0k
Layer 2   100c 0m 50y 0k

3
Layer 1   70c 60m 60y 50k
Layer 2   30c 20m 40y 0k

2

3

Art Nouveau

France, 1897

CD: **43 Art Nouveau.eps**

Swiss-born Eugène Grasset worked across many artistic disciplines, but he is best known for his landmark publication *La Plante et ses Applications Ornementales*, from which this pattern derives. His philosophy of viewing design as 'a way of expressing our joy in living' exemplified one Art Nouveau ideal, one that is amply demonstrated through the sensitively executed forms found in this delightful periwinkle pattern.

1

1

Layer 1	50c 20m 60y 0k
Layer 2	70c 20m 10y 0k
Layer 3	40c 10m 10y 0k
Layer 4	30c 10m 40y 0k
Layer 5	0c 5m 40y 0k
Layer 6	100c 70m 80y 0k

2

Layer 1	90c 10m 40y 0k
Layer 2	0c 70m 30y 0k
Layer 3	10c 100m 80y 0k
Layer 4	30c 10m 20y 0k
Layer 5	30c 40m 20y 0k
Layer 6	80c 70m 80y 0k

3

Layer 1	60c 70m 80y 0k
Layer 2	60c 80m 30y 0k
Layer 3	0c 90m 50y 0k
Layer 4	0c 70m 90y 0k
Layer 5	10c 30m 60y 0k
Layer 6	90c 80m 60y 0k

2

3

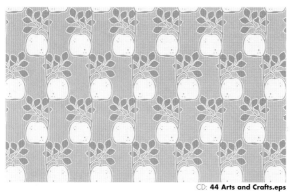

Arts and Crafts
Britain, 1900

Created by Lindsay P
Butterfield at the dawn of
the twentieth century, and
produced as a block-printed
linen, this pattern has an
appealing simplicity and
a lightness of touch given
cohesion by the gently
undulating branches, which
echo the Chinese continuous-
stem convention. The Arts
and Crafts movement cared
little for slavish fidelity to
nature's hues, and this blue
apple will be equally
pleasing whatever its colour.

1
Layer 1   30c 5m 0y 0k
Layer 2   60c 20m 0y 30k
Layer 3   0c 0m 0y 0k
Layer 4   50c 20m 5y 0k

2
Layer 1   60c 80m 40y 0k
Layer 2   80c 90m 80y 20k
Layer 3   0c 0m 0y 0k
Layer 4   70c 50m 30y 0k

3
Layer 1   60c 30m 50y 0k
Layer 2   80c 60m 90y 0k
Layer 3   0c 0m 0y 0k
Layer 4   20c 40m 60y 0k

1

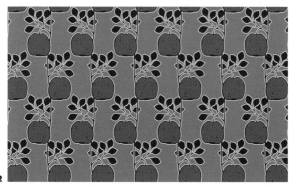

2

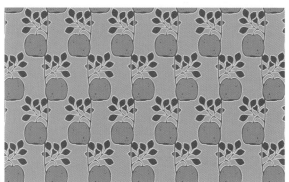

3

Arts and Crafts

Britain, 1909

Lyrical, fluid movement was central to the Arts and Crafts style, as exemplified in this pattern by Harry Napper, which was used on a block-printed cotton. The subject matter enjoys a sense of sturdy well-being through the confident line work, and this linear robustness will support the palest of infilling. Alternatively, the use of primary colours may reveal a design reminiscent of stained-glass work.

1
Layer 1   20c 10m 20y 0k
Layer 2   100c 100m 40y 0k
Layer 3   30c 5m 0y 10k

2
Layer 1   20c 40m 70y 0k
Layer 2   80c 70m 80y 10k
Layer 3   50c 80m 80y 0k

3
Layer 1   0c 20m 100y 0k
Layer 2   100c 0m 20y 0k
Layer 3   0c 100m 100y 0k

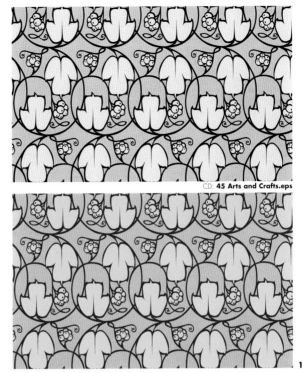

CD: **45 Arts and Crafts.eps**

1

2

3

1

2

3

Modern

France, 1924

This simple floral pattern was included in the respected publication *Etoffes et Papiers Peints*, published in Paris. Contrary to compositional convention, the leaves here have more prominence than the flower heads, making this an unusual image and arguably adding to its undeniable charm. The leaves can be allowed to recede into the ground to rebalance the pattern, if such an effect is desired.

1
Layer 1   10c 40m 30y 0k
Layer 2   0c 0m 0y 100k
Layer 3   5c 10m 20y 0k

2
Layer 1   20c 100m 0y 0k
Layer 2   80c 90m 90y 0k
Layer 3   0c 50m 100y 0k

3
Layer 1   70c 90m 80y 10k
Layer 2   80c 50m 80y 20k
Layer 3   40c 20m 30y 0k

Art Deco

France, 1927

The French artist Serge
Gladky was working
halfway between the two
disciplines of representation
and abstraction with this
bold fish design, which was
included in the influential
*Nouvelles Compositions
Decoratives*, published in
Paris. Gladky's colour
choices may have been
playful, in that they could
hardly be less aquatic.
However, this pattern would
look equally handsome with
some greenish-blues.

CD: **47 Art Deco.eps**

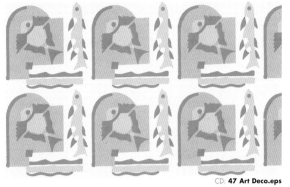

1
Layer 1   40c 20m 20y 0k
Layer 2   40c 30m 50y 0k
Layer 3   0c 40m 30y 0k
Layer 4   5c 5m 40y 0k

2
Layer 1   80c 30m 20y 0k
Layer 2   50c 50m 50y 100k
Layer 3   30c 100m 70y 0k
Layer 4   20c 10m 10y 0k

3
Layer 1   70c 40m 0y 0k
Layer 2   60c 90m 40y 0k
Layer 3   80c 50m 60y 0k
Layer 4   0c 40m 20y 0k

1

2

3

47

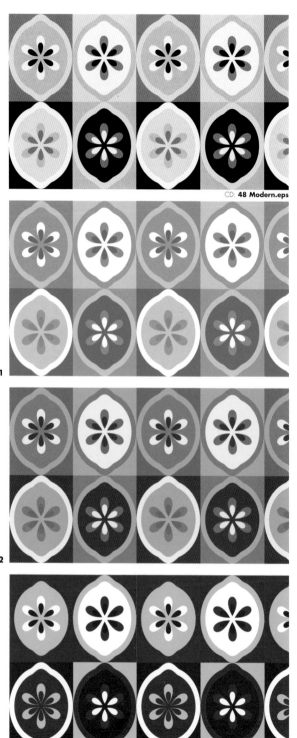

CD: **48 Modern.eps**

Modern
Britain, 2003

Western fabric-design
work of the 1950s informs
this design, which features
lemon motifs with a
decidedly uncitric palette.
There is perhaps a longer
historical lineage in this
regard: throughout the
history of decorative
art, recognizable forms
have regularly been
afforded a different
dimension by the use of
unexpected colourways.
Certainly, patterns can
amuse as well as decorate.

1
Layer 1   60c 30m 30y 0k
Layer 2   50c 5m 0y 0k
Layer 3   50c 70m 90y 0k
Layer 4   20c 60m 100y 0k
Layer 5   0c 0m 0y 0k

2
Layer 1   10c 80m 30y 0k
Layer 2   70c 10m 20y 0k
Layer 3   80c 80m 80y 20k
Layer 4   70c 70m 10y 0k
Layer 5   0c 10m 30y 0k

3
Layer 1   50c 0m 100y 0k
Layer 2   0c 100m 0y 0k
Layer 3   90c 100m 0y 0k
Layer 4   40c 100m 30y 0k
Layer 5   0c 0m 0y 0k

Modern

Britain, 2003

Although this pattern borrows its expansive ovoid shapes from 1930s design and its fruity subject matter from postwar decorative trends, the brown and mustard colours of these kiwi fruits bring them firmly into the twenty-first century. Styles and motifs from pattern design's rich legacy are forever being recycled and reinterpreted as part of the evolution of the craft.

CD: **49 Modern.eps**

1

1
Layer 1   0c 0m 0y 0k
Layer 2   0c 5m 20y 0k
Layer 3   60c 80m 60y 0k
Layer 4   10c 20m 40y 0k
Layer 5   20c 30m 60y 0k

2
Layer 1   0c 0m 0y 0k
Layer 2   40c 40m 40y 0k
Layer 3   70c 60m 30y 60k
Layer 4   60c 10m 40y 0k
Layer 5   70c 70m 50y 0k

3
Layer 1   0c 0m 0y 0k
Layer 2   0c 30m 80y 0k
Layer 3   80c 90m 90y 10k
Layer 4   0c 70m 90y 0k
Layer 5   70c 60m 90y 0k

2

3

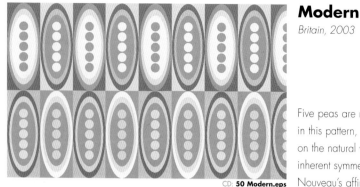

CD: **50 Modern.eps**

Modern
Britain, 2003

Five peas are neatly aligned in this pattern, which draws on the natural world's inherent symmetry. Art Nouveau's affinity with nature, Art Deco's geometric conventions and the exuberant, colourful decorative work of the 1960s can all be seen as influential here. Steering the colours away from green toward red will produce a more abstract design.

1

1
Layer 1	80c 20m 70y 0k
Layer 2	60c 0m 10y 0k
Layer 3	50c 0m 70y 0k
Layer 4	30c 10m 70y 0k
Layer 5	0c 0m 0y 0k
Layer 6	0c 10m 80y 0k

2
Layer 1	70c 70m 50y 0k
Layer 2	70c 50m 10y 0k
Layer 3	90c 60m 80y 0k
Layer 4	0c 90m 50y 0k
Layer 5	0c 0m 0y 0k
Layer 6	10c 30m 60y 0k

3
Layer 1	80c 0m 20y 0k
Layer 2	60c 0m 30y 0k
Layer 3	80c 40m 10y 0k
Layer 4	0c 50m 10y 0k
Layer 5	10c 10m 20y 0k
Layer 6	50c 30m 30y 0k

2

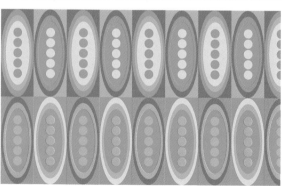

3

Modern

Britain, 2003

The strong connection between music and the natural world is explored in this flowing repeat pattern, in which natural forms lend lyrical movement to the guitar, and the shapes become one. The influence of 1940s and 1950s graphic work can be detected in the uniform line weights above the misaligned blocks of colour, but altering the palette gives a distinctly different atmosphere.

CD: **51 Modern.eps**

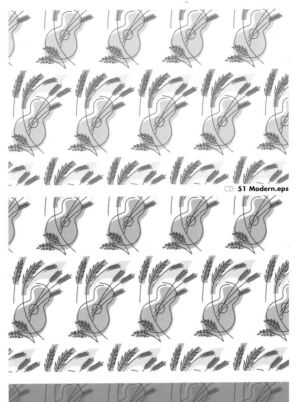

1

1
Layer 1   30c 80m 50y 30k
Layer 2   50c 20m 10y 0k
Layer 3   20c 5m 10y 0k
Layer 4   20c 30m 30y 0k
Layer 5   0c 0m 0y 0k

2
Layer 1   90c 60m 40y 0k
Layer 2   40c 50m 80y 0k
Layer 3   40c 30m 40y 0k
Layer 4   60c 50m 10y 0k
Layer 5   60c 30m 30y 0k

3
Layer 1   0c 0m 0y 100k
Layer 2   0c 100m 50y 0k
Layer 3   0c 20m 90y 0k
Layer 4   30c 0m 100y 0k
Layer 5   0c 0m 0y 0k

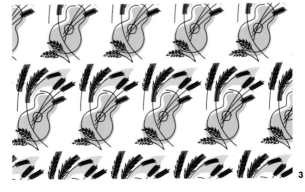

2

3

CD: **52 Ancient World.eps**

1

2

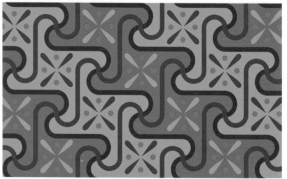

3

Ancient World

Egypt, c.1000 BC

The writing system of hieroglyphics conveyed complex ideas and beliefs through simple pictures and symbols; this decorative painted pattern signifies the rolling waves of the sea and the abundance therein. The availability of natural pigments meant that red, blue and yellow were dominant, but with a racier palette, this design may resemble a mid-twentieth-century work, such is its graphic strength.

1

Layer 1	70c 90m 90y 0k
Layer 2	0c 0m 0y 0k
Layer 3	0c 20m 100y 0k
Layer 4	60c 20m 20y 0k
Layer 5	0c 0m 0y 100k
Layer 6	70c 90m 90y 0k
Layer 7	0c 100m 100y 0k
Layer 8	100c 0m 0y 0k

2

Layer 1	0c 0m 0y 0k
Layer 2	0c 0m 0y 0k
Layer 3	40c 0m 90y 0k
Layer 4	40c 0m 90y 0k
Layer 5	80c 100m 0y 0k
Layer 6	100c 40m 100y 0k
Layer 7	0c 90m 90y 0k
Layer 8	40c 100m 0y 0k

3

Layer 1	0c 80m 90y 0k
Layer 2	0c 80m 90y 0k
Layer 3	10c 50m 90y 0k
Layer 4	100c 80m 40y 0k
Layer 5	100c 80m 40y 0k
Layer 6	60c 100m 40y 0k
Layer 7	10c 50m 90y 0k
Layer 8	50c 70m 90y 0k

Ancient World

Egypt, c.1000 BC

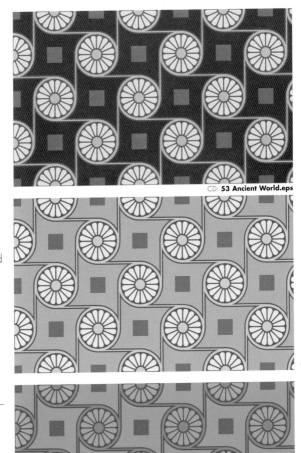

CD: **53 Ancient World.eps**

Flower buds are placed within the enduring Egyptian coiled-rope symbol on this painting from a mummy case, and the whole becomes representative of nature's cyclical continuity and generative power. Symbols such as these lasted through various epochs, alongside others invested with similar universal meaning. Used at a small size, this repeat will have a refined, dignified quality.

1
Layer 1 30c 80m 60y 0k
Layer 2 5c 5m 30y 0k
Layer 3 50c 90m 60y 0k
Layer 4 10c 20m 40y 0k
Layer 5 30c 30m 60y 0k

2
Layer 1 0c 90m 10y 0k
Layer 2 0c 50m 90y 0k
Layer 3 90c 80m 0y 0k
Layer 4 50c 50m 90y 0k
Layer 5 80c 0m 50y 0k

3
Layer 1 60c 20m 30y 0k
Layer 2 30c 40m 40y 0k
Layer 3 70c 60m 10y 0k
Layer 4 20c 30m 60y 0k
Layer 5 50c 60m 20y 0k

1

2

3

Ancient World
Egypt, c.1000 BC

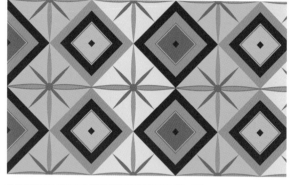

CD: **54 Ancient World.eps**

A graceful symmetry and inventive colour distribution distinguish this painted pattern featuring palm leaves, which comes from the ceiling of a tomb. The date was among the most venerated of plant forms in the ancient world; its fruit provided nourishment for body and mind, and its other constituents yielded materials for building and crafts. There is endless scope for colour interpretation with this versatile pattern.

1
Layer 1   30c 80m 60y 0k
Layer 2   60c 20m 60y 0k
Layer 3   80c 100m 30y 0k
Layer 4   10c 5m 40y 0k
Layer 5   10c 30m 60y 0k
Layer 6   80c 100m 30y 0k

2
Layer 1   20c 10m 80y 0k
Layer 2   60c 50m 0y 0k
Layer 3   70c 100m 70y 0k
Layer 4   60c 0m 40y 0k
Layer 5   0c 70m 80y 0k
Layer 6   70c 100m 70y 0k

3
Layer 1   70c 60m 60y 0k
Layer 2   80c 50m 40y 20k
Layer 3   100c 70m 30y 50k
Layer 4   30c 30m 30y 30k
Layer 5   30c 30m 30y 30k
Layer 6   10c 20m 40y 0k

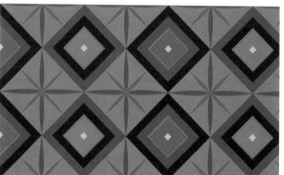

1

2

3

Victorian

Britain, c.1850

Unusually geometric for the Victorian period, this pattern was published as a design suitable for the decoration of a dado, or lower part of an interior wall. The original's colour combination of khaki, yellow and cool grey is not immediately harmonious, but the addition of black helps unify the pattern. Colour experimentation is key to getting the most from this adventurous design.

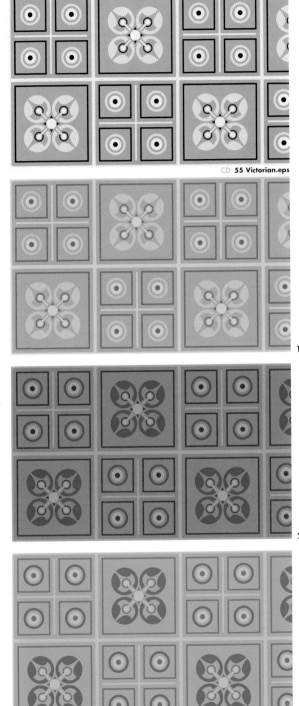

CD: **55 Victorian.eps**

1

1
Layer 1	30c 20m 20y 0k
Layer 2	70c 70m 60y 0k
Layer 3	10c 20m 50y 0k
Layer 4	30c 40m 60y 0k

2
Layer 1	60c 90m 90y 0k
Layer 2	80c 80m 10y 50k
Layer 3	20c 40m 50y 10k
Layer 4	70c 50m 30y 0k

3
Layer 1	100c 40m 40y 0k
Layer 2	90c 40m 40y 0k
Layer 3	40c 0m 100y 0k
Layer 4	70c 0m 50y 0k

2

3

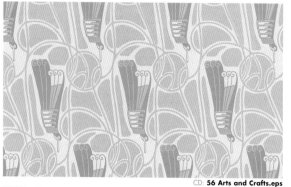

Arts and Crafts
France, 1906

A fan-like symbol is the focus of this pattern for woven silk designed by Georges de Feure, which also features the sinuous shapes synonymous with the Art Nouveau movement. Ochres and greyish-browns impart a rich, earthy feel to this abstraction. Through colour manipulation, the main form can be modelled to appear suggestive of breaking waves.

CD: **56 Arts and Crafts.eps**

1

1
Layer 1 50c 50m 60y 0k
Layer 2 20c 40m 60y 0k
Layer 3 10c 20m 40y 0k

2
Layer 1 60c 50m 10y 0k
Layer 2 90c 60m 40y 0k
Layer 3 60c 30m 30y 0k

3
Layer 1 90c 100m 0y 0k
Layer 2 100c 0m 40y 0k
Layer 3 0c 90m 10y 0k

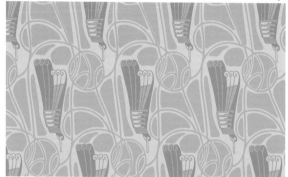

2

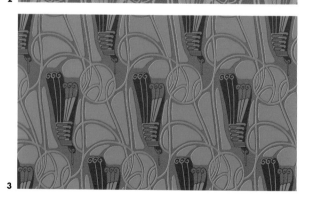

3

Art Deco

Russia, c.1920

The bold line work on this printed cotton design from the Serpulov factory lends a real immediacy to its motifs, which represent communication through electrical energy. The style is reminiscent of coarse woodcut, which adds to the pattern's graphic vitality. The well-judged colours are infinitely pliable: closer contrast values will yield a more abstract and less representational effect.

1
Layer 1   50c 20m 50y 0k
Layer 2   5c 50m 60y 0k
Layer 3   60c 50m 50y 0k
Layer 4   10c 5m 10y 0k

2
Layer 1   0c 60m 80y 0k
Layer 2   20c 70m 0y 0k
Layer 3   80c 0m 50y 0k
Layer 4   0c 0m 70y 0k

3
Layer 1   60c 0m 20y 0k
Layer 2   80c 60m 30y 0k
Layer 3   60c 70m 80y 0k
Layer 4   10c 10m 30y 0k

CD: **57 Art Deco.eps**

1

2

3

CD: **58 Art Deco.eps**

Art Deco
France, 1925

Various influences from the history of pattern design can be detected in this gestural abstract work, including the Egyptians' formal, balanced distribution of objects and the Chinese tendency to create a unifying link between repeats. It was created by E A Seguy and published in his *Suggestions pour Etoffes et Tapis*. Allowing reds and greens to dominate here will introduce a festive note.

1
Layer 1   60c 10m 50y 0k
Layer 2   90c 40m 40y 0k
Layer 3   5c 40m 50y 0k
Layer 4   20c 90m 50y 0k
Layer 5   0c 20m 40y 0k
Layer 6   0c 0m 0y 0k

2
Layer 1   80c 90m 80y 20k
Layer 2   50c 80m 40y 0k
Layer 3   60c 40m 40y 0k
Layer 4   100c 100m 50y 0k
Layer 5   30c 30m 10y 0k
Layer 6   10c 50m 30y 0k

3
Layer 1   90c 40m 50y 40k
Layer 2   90c 0m 80y 0k
Layer 3   10c 90m 20y 0k
Layer 4   100c 40m 90y 0k
Layer 5   30c 100m 90y 0k
Layer 6   30c 10m 70y 0k

Art Deco
France, 1925

A bold curve provides the counterpoint to the harder geometric forms in this imaginative pattern, which is part of the *Kaleidoscope* folio of designs. The publication of this work was the culmination of Maurice Verneuil's aesthetic odyssey. Despite the flat rendering and the presence of the same colours in front and behind, the composition has a distinct sense of depth, which may be further exploited using alternative palettes.

CD: **59 Art Deco.eps**

1

1
Layer 1	90c 40m 0y 0k
Layer 2	0c 90m 40y 0k
Layer 3	60c 80m 0y 0k
Layer 4	0c 0m 20y 0k
Layer 5	60c 0m 20y 0k

2
Layer 1	0c 0m 0y 100k
Layer 2	30c 100m 0y 0k
Layer 3	90c 90m 0y 0k
Layer 4	0c 90m 10y 0k
Layer 5	30c 0m 90y 0k

3
Layer 1	80c 60m 30y 0k
Layer 2	30c 50m 70y 0k
Layer 3	50c 40m 40y 0k
Layer 4	0c 10m 40y 0k
Layer 5	10c 30m 30y 0k

2

3

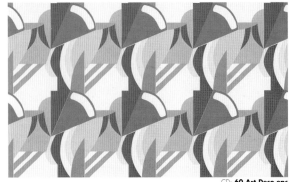

Art Deco
France, 1925

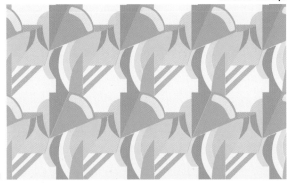

CD: **60 Art Deco.eps**

As a pupil of that great master of organic representation, Eugène Grasset, Maurice Verneuil regularly used the shapes and tones of nature in his patterns, even as his work became increasingly abstract. The fruits of summer can be seen in the wedges and curves of this repeat design, whose zesty, upbeat colours are punctuated by two contrasting pink stripes.

1

Layer 1	40c 0m 20y 0k
Layer 2	50c 0m 5y 0k
Layer 3	0c 50m 60y 0k
Layer 4	60c 0m 90y 0k
Layer 5	0c 10m 100y 0k
Layer 6	25c 0m 15y 0k
Layer 7	70c 0m 40y 0k
Layer 8	70c 20m 0y 0k
Layer 9	0c 5m 30y 0k

2

Layer 1	30c 100m 10y 0k
Layer 2	0c 20m 100y 0k
Layer 3	0c 50m 100y 0k
Layer 4	100c 90m 0y 0k
Layer 5	100c 0m 100y 0k
Layer 6	0c 80m 90y 0k
Layer 7	10c 100m 100y 0k
Layer 8	50c 50m 50y 100k
Layer 9	100c 30m 0y 0k

3

Layer 1	0c 70m 20y 0k
Layer 2	50c 30m 40y 0k
Layer 3	30c 40m 20y 0k
Layer 4	90c 0m 50y 0k
Layer 5	40c 0m 10y 0k
Layer 6	50c 30m 0y 0k
Layer 7	70c 60m 0y 0k
Layer 8	0c 0m 0y 70k
Layer 9	90c 60m 50y 0k

1

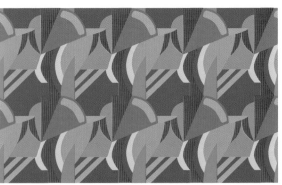

2

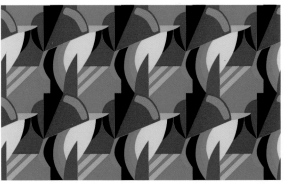

3

Art Deco

France, 1925

When oriented as its creator intended (as shown here), a human figure engaged in a task can be seen in this pattern. Turned 90 degrees counterclockwise, however, the design might suggest laboratory equipment. Different forms emerge when a design is looked at afresh, or when a new palette is applied, such are the delights of ingenious abstractions such as this.

CD: **61 Art Deco.eps**

1

1

Layer 1   50c 20m 0y 10k
Layer 2   0c 10m 100y 0k
Layer 3   0c 0m 0y 30k
Layer 4   0c 50m 0y 100k
Layer 5   0c 60m 90y 0k

2

Layer 1   80c 70m 90y 0k
Layer 2   0c 30m 90y 0k
Layer 3   30c 40m 90y 0k
Layer 4   0c 0m 0y 100k
Layer 5   40c 60m 90y 0k

3

Layer 1   80c 0m 40y 0k
Layer 2   40c 50m 70y 0k
Layer 3   0c 10m 30y 0k
Layer 4   80c 80m 40y 20k
Layer 5   0c 90m 90y 0k

2

3

CD: **62 Modern.eps**

Modern
USA, 1927

The Stehli Silk Corporation was prominent in the creation of boundary-pushing designs that helped introduce a new vocabulary to pattern design. This example on a printed crêpe de Chine has a confident patriotic swagger, and it's hard to resist interpreting these motifs as fireworks over a vigorous 1920s urban scene. A dark blue ground does not diminish the impact of this pattern in the least.

1

1
Layer 1   30c 80m 70y 0k
Layer 2   0c 20m 50y 0k
Layer 3   90c 90m 50y 50k

2
Layer 1   0c 10m 100y 0k
Layer 2   100c 100m 0y 0k
Layer 3   100c 0m 20y 0k

3
Layer 1   90c 0m 50y 0k
Layer 2   0c 80m 0y 0k
Layer 3   100c 80m 0y 0k

2

3
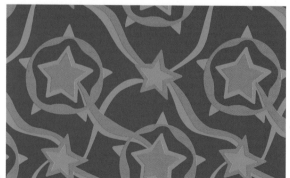

Art Deco
Britain, 1928

This classic geometric pattern was used on book endpapers by the Curwen Press, derived from a design by Paul Nash. Its execution shows the influence of wood engraving, a medium to which Nash was no stranger, while the moody, muted colourway is redolent of African decorative art. The approximated perspective adds an element of illusion: this pattern hints at other forms when it is oriented differently.

1
Layer 1   80c 100m 70y 0k
Layer 2   20c 20m 40y 0k
Layer 3   0c 10m 40y 0k

2
Layer 1   90c 100m 0y 0k
Layer 2   20c 100m 0y 0k
Layer 3   0c 60m 100y 0k

3
Layer 1   100c 60m 0y 0k
Layer 2   60c 0m 30y 0k
Layer 3   90c 0m 10y 0k

CD: **63 Art Deco.eps**

1

2

3

63

CD: **64 Art Deco.eps**

Art Deco
France, 1929

This bold geometric pattern was found on a textile designed by the prolific French artist Serge Gladky. It can be interpreted as the roofs and windows of a series of buildings or seen purely as an abstraction. Experimentation with colour will produce results with various levels of abstraction, and a restricted or even monochromatic colourway will bring a more highly textured effect to the design.

1

1
Layer 1   50c 0m 60y 0k
Layer 2   0c 75m 0y 0k
Layer 3   0c 0m 0y 100k
Layer 4   0c 0m 10y 0k

2
Layer 1   40c 20m 30y 0k
Layer 2   70c 60m 90y 0k
Layer 3   80c 50m 80y 0k
Layer 4   10c 10m 30y 0k

3
Layer 1   0c 10m 85y 0k
Layer 2   0c 0m 0y 0k
Layer 3   90c 35m 0y 30k
Layer 4   0c 10m 10y 15k

2

3

Art Deco

France, 1930

The intriguing motif at the heart of this abstract design can be seen as any number of things: a multistory building, a T-square, and a coffee machine are three that may spring to mind. The wavy lines somewhat soften the appearance of the otherwise hard, abutting shapes of this pattern, which nevertheless remains curiously elegant and stylistically very much of its time and origin.

CD: **65 Art Deco.eps**

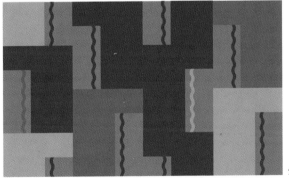

1

1
Layer 1   60c 10m 80y 0k
Layer 2   10c 0m 80y 0k
Layer 3   0c 0m 0y 100k
Layer 4   0c 0m 0y 0k
Layer 5   20c 0m 0y 30k

2
Layer 1   80c 60m 80y 0k
Layer 2   40c 40m 40y 0k
Layer 3   90c 80m 60y 10k
Layer 4   70c 90m 50y 10k
Layer 5   60c 60m 60y 0k

3
Layer 1   80c 0m 20y 0k
Layer 2   30c 30m 30y 0k
Layer 3   90c 90m 0y 0k
Layer 4   20c 40m 80y 0k
Layer 5   0c 70m 90y 0k

2

3

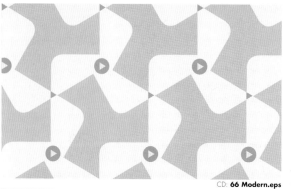

Modern
Britain, 2004

Suggestive of wind turbines, this pattern is evocative of both the more linear Japanese decorative art and the formal disposition of Islamic work. The motif is based on the division of a circle into three, which yields an equilateral triangle as each of the axes is shifted from the fulcrum. The colours in these examples may suggest uses for this simple small repeat.

CD: **66 Modern.eps**

1

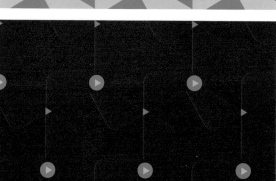

1
Layer 1   90c 10m 40y 0k
Layer 2   40c 80m 20y 0k
Layer 3   0c 20m 80y 0k
Layer 4   50c 0m 20y 0k

2
Layer 1   0c 100m 0y 0k
Layer 2   100c 0m 50y 0k
Layer 3   50c 0m 100y 0k
Layer 4   90c 100m 0y 0k

3
Layer 1   50c 0m 0y 100k
Layer 2   20c 60m 100y 0k
Layer 3   0c 0m 0y 0k
Layer 4   70c 30m 40y 0k

2

3

Modern
Britain, 2004

The rapid pace of modern life and the analogous flow of data transfer are two ideas suggested by this modern pattern. The arrow was popular in the symbolically adventurous commercial art of the 1960s, as were clashing colours, which here introduce a sense of ordered chaos. This visual discord may be mitigated by working within only a narrow band of the colour spectrum.

CD: **67 Modern.eps**

1

1
Layer 1   60c 60m 0y 0k
Layer 2   0c 0m 100y 0k
Layer 3   100c 10m 0y 0k
Layer 4   100c 100m 0y 0k

2
Layer 1   40c 10m 0y 50k
Layer 2   50c 10m 20y 0k
Layer 3   100c 60m 40y 10k
Layer 4   60c 40m 40y 0k

3
Layer 1   50c 0m 0y 100k
Layer 2   0c 0m 0y 0k
Layer 3   60c 100m 40y 0k
Layer 4   20c 60m 100y 0k

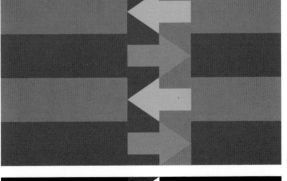

2

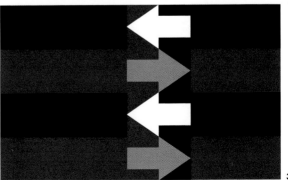

3

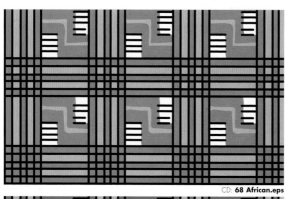

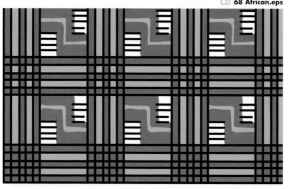

African
Traditional

Pigments derived from naturally occurring local sources define the prevailing colour palettes found in African decorative art, hence the rich, earthy tones of this cloth sample. With its linear interlacing and asymmetrical detailing, the well-judged repeat composition is poised yet robust, and the teeth-like detail within the repeats may be symbolic, though of what one can only speculate.

CD: **68 African.eps**

1
Layer 1 0c 0m 0y 100k
Layer 2 5c 30m 100y 0k
Layer 3 0c 0m 0y 0k
Layer 4 30c 70m 100y 0k

2
Layer 1 100c 90m 40y 10k
Layer 2 100c 20m 20y 0k
Layer 3 0c 100m 90y 0k
Layer 4 30c 100m 0y 0k

3
Layer 1 70c 100m 0y 0k
Layer 2 20c 20m 20y 0k
Layer 3 0c 90m 10y 0k
Layer 4 0c 80m 100y 0k

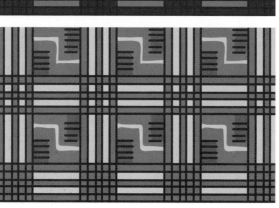

South American

Mexico, Traditional

This pattern is adapted from the embroidered border of a woman's skirt, and it is one example of the needlework craft of the Mexican Huichol women. Animals often feature in their decorative art, and this scene of a cat chasing fleeing birds may be a vignette from a folktale. The vibrant, joyful colours of the original are characteristic of much pattern work from Mexico.

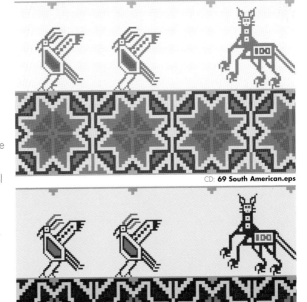

CD: **69 South American.eps**

1

Layer 1   0c 60m 100y 0k
Layer 2   0c 20m 100y 0k
Layer 3   100c 0m 100y 0k
Layer 4   0c 100m 100y 0k
Layer 5   100c 100m 0y 0k
Layer 6   0c 10m 30y 0k

2

Layer 1   30c 40m 40y 0k
Layer 2   50c 70m 100y 0k
Layer 3   40c 100m 70y 0k
Layer 4   70c 100m 60y 0k
Layer 5   100c 100m 50y 0k
Layer 6   30c 20m 40y 0k

3

Layer 1   0c 50m 100y 0k
Layer 2   10c 100m 0y 0k
Layer 3   0c 50m 100y 0k
Layer 4   100c 30m 0y 0k
Layer 5   0c 0m 0y 100k
Layer 6   0c 10m 40y 0k

1

2

3

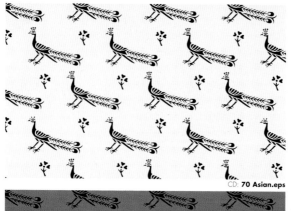

CD: **70 Asian.eps**

1

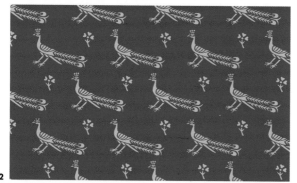

2

3

Asian

India, Traditional

Floor decorations called *sanzi* may be found in Indian temples on festive occasions. These vibrant designs are created with stencils, or *khaka*, and powdered colours, and their painstaking creation yet ephemeral existence is a measure of the importance of decoration in Hindu culture. The peacock has a special place in Indian symbolism, and this proud-looking creature will look splendid in any colourway.

1
Layer 1   50c 0m 0y 100k
Layer 2   20c 30m 40y 50k

2
Layer 1   50c 0m 30y 0k
Layer 2   100c 70m 10y 0k

3
Layer 1   0c 50m 30y 0k
Layer 2   80c 50m 60y 50k

Asian

India, Traditional

The exotic birds in this pattern are seen to be guarding a lush plant form in a composition typical of India. Such traditional designs may be found across many different crafts, such as embroidery, weaving, and fabric printing. The greyish-blues here may be replaced by more vibrant oranges, and using the pattern at a large size can create a more iconic effect.

CD: **71 Asian.eps**

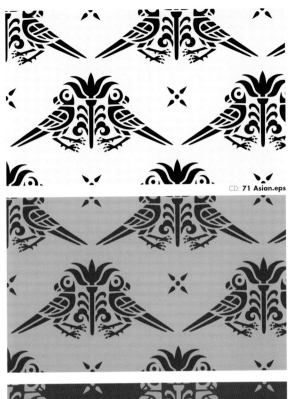

1
Layer 1   70c 100m 20y 0k
Layer 2   0c 50m 100y 0k

2
Layer 1   70c 0m 50y 0k
Layer 2   100c 50m 10y 50k

3
Layer 1   50c 30m 20y 40k
Layer 2   0c 10m 50y 0k

1

2

3

CD: **72 Australasian.eps**

1

2

3

Australasian
Australia, Traditional

The style of Australian Aboriginal patterns that we immediately recognize today was established long before the arrival of European settlers. The tradition was artistically sensitive and adept, informed by a strong sense of oneness with the natural world, and its themes and motifs are still in use. Through the use of different background colours, this design may variously suggest stellar constellations or waves.

1
Layer 1 10c 30m 100y 0k
Layer 2 40c 30m 100y 0k
Layer 3 50c 100m 100y 0k

2
Layer 1 10c 100m 0y 0k
Layer 2 20c 0m 100y 10k
Layer 3 50c 0m 0y 100k

3
Layer 1 20c 30m 40y 50k
Layer 2 50c 0m 0y 100k
Layer 3 70c 30m 40y 0k

Polynesian
Traditional

Much Polynesian pattern work is pure decoration, but it is easy to see the aquatic influence in the shapes and motifs traditionally used by the islanders in a region where the ocean is such a basic influence on daily life. These delicate designs are suggestive of the ocean and marine life, and may be rendered luminous by colour contrasts or made subtly textural with closer hues.

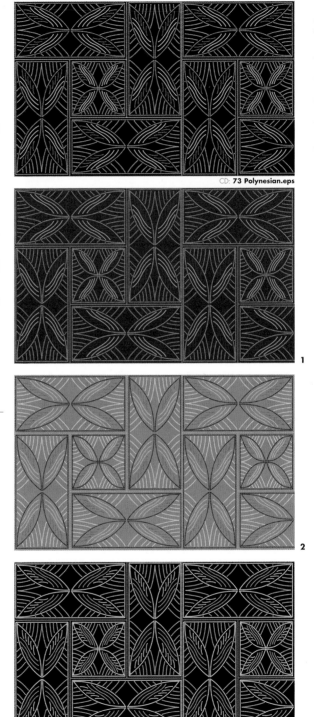

CD: **73 Polynesian.eps**

1

2

3

1
Layer 1	70c 0m 100y 0k
Layer 2	0c 20m 100y 0k
Layer 3	0c 100m 100y 0k
Layer 4	0c 50m 100y 0k
Layer 5	50c 50m 0y 0k
Layer 6	100c 100m 0y 0k

2
Layer 1	0c 50m 30y 0k
Layer 2	50c 0m 30y 0k
Layer 3	40c 70m 70y 0k
Layer 4	50c 0m 0y 100k
Layer 5	0c 10m 40y 0k
Layer 6	40c 10m 0y 50k

3
Layer 1	0c 0m 0y 50k
Layer 2	0c 50m 30y 0k
Layer 3	0c 10m 50y 0k
Layer 4	0c 0m 0y 0k
Layer 5	50c 0m 20y 0k
Layer 6	0c 0m 0y 100k

Modern
Britain, 2003

The nine birds that comprise this pattern seem to be absorbed in attentive avian discourse. Their naïve style can be compared to much traditional folk art from around the world, while the square grid observes more formal design practices. The absence of superfluous detail here confers an almost symbolic quality to each figure within this friendly and versatile design.

CD: **74 Modern.eps**

1
Layer 1	0c 80m 100y 0k
Layer 2	0c 0m 0y 0k
Layer 3	0c 80m 100y 0k
Layer 4	0c 0m 0y 100k

2
Layer 1	40c 100m 60y 50k
Layer 2	70c 30m 40y 0k
Layer 3	90c 100m 30y 10k
Layer 4	60c 50m 50y 0k

3
Layer 1	70c 0m 100y 0k
Layer 2	0c 0m 0y 0k
Layer 3	0c 50m 100y 0k
Layer 4	100c 70m 0y 0k

1

2

3

Polynesian
Tonga, Traditional

The border of a Tongan dress is the basis of this pattern. The fabric was traditionally made from the inner bark of a tree, beaten until thin and pliable, and then decorated with small stamps of contrasting wood to create the detail. The precision is remarkable given these rudimentary production techniques, and the predominance of black gives the design a dense, evocative feeling.

CD: **75 Polynesian.eps**

1
Layer 1   0c 0m 0y 100k
Layer 2   10c 20m 50y 0k

2
Layer 1   0c 50m 10y 0k
Layer 2   70c 60m 30y 50k

3
Layer 1   40c 70m 50y 30k
Layer 2   50c 0m 30y 0k

1

2

3

CD: **76 African.eps**

African
Traditional

Fabric patterns like this can be found all over the African continent, with variations in colour and style from country to country. The details here serve simply as decoration in most African societies, but in some areas they are still invested with more symbolic significance, such as tribal identity. This rich design demands a bright combination of colours.

1

1

Layer 1	70c 0m 70y 0k
Layer 2	80c 0m 10y 0k
Layer 3	100c 50m 0y 0k
Layer 4	50c 100m 0y 0k
Layer 5	70c 0m 70y 0k
Layer 6	100c 100m 0y 0k

2

Layer 1	70c 80m 80y 0k
Layer 2	80c 60m 10y 0k
Layer 3	0c 90m 30y 0k
Layer 4	30c 100m 0y 0k
Layer 5	100c 80m 50y 0k
Layer 6	20c 40m 80y 0k

2

3

Layer 1	60c 50m 0y 0k
Layer 2	0c 70m 80y 0k
Layer 3	60c 0m 80y 0k
Layer 4	40c 80m 10y 0k
Layer 5	0c 60m 30y 0k
Layer 6	70c 100m 70y 0k

3

Native American

USA, Traditional

The indigenous peoples of North America foster a rich visual tradition in which the many features of the natural world they hold sacred are represented by a host of symbols. The zigzags in this pattern are symbolic of mountains, while the crosses represent the sacred morning star, bringer of hope and courage. This is a design to consider for making a bold graphic statement.

CD: **77 Native American.eps**

1

1

Layer 1   40c 30m 40y 0k
Layer 2   50c 40m 30y 30k
Layer 3   100c 80m 50y 0k
Layer 4   50c 40m 30y 30k
Layer 5   0c 0m 0y 100k

2

Layer 1   0c 30m 100y 0k
Layer 2   80c 100m 0y 0k
Layer 3   0c 100m 0y 0k
Layer 4   30c 100m 0y 0k
Layer 5   80c 100m 0y 0k

3

Layer 1   10c 20m 40y 0k
Layer 2   70c 40m 30y 0k
Layer 3   100c 70m 30y 50k
Layer 4   70c 40m 50y 0k
Layer 5   70c 90m 50y 10k

2

3

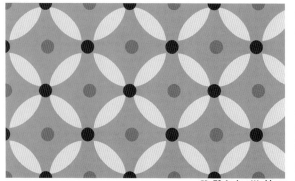

CD: **78 Ancient World.eps**

Ancient World
Egypt, c.1000 BC

Archetypal Egyptian work
from an ancient tomb, this
balanced, well-proportioned
pattern is delicate and
unassuming, making it
perfect for an application
that demands a discreet,
ordered, small repeat.
The red and yellow ochre
of the original could be
replaced with blues for
a cooler look, or the black
reversed out of a darker
ground to enhance the
floral aspect.

1

1
Layer 1 30c 60m 100y 0k
Layer 2 80c 90m 100y 0k
Layer 3 10c 40m 100y 0k
Layer 4 30c 100m 100y 0k

2
Layer 1 60c 30m 40y 0k
Layer 2 90c 50m 40y 0k
Layer 3 30c 20m 20y 0k
Layer 4 50c 20m 20y 0k

3
Layer 1 0c 90m 70y 0k
Layer 2 60c 90m 90y 0k
Layer 3 80c 60m 90y 0k
Layer 4 20c 30m 40y 0k

2

3

Indo-Persian

c.1400

This small repeating pattern can be traced to a mural painted in the early fifteenth century. It features two different floral devices that are symmetrically drafted, tastefully spaced, and plainly coloured. Victorian decorative conventions echoed such formal practices, and designs in this ancient style enjoyed a nineteenth-century revival. This infinitely flexible pattern may evoke either era through experimentation with different colour combinations.

1
Layer 1	0c 50m 75y 10k
Layer 2	0c 15m 55y 0k
Layer 3	50c 30m 0y 35k
Layer 4	0c 100m 100y 0k

2
Layer 1	0c 20m 75y 15k
Layer 2	0c 100m 100y 0k
Layer 3	0c 0m 0y 0k
Layer 4	50c 30m 0y 35k

3
Layer 1	0c 20m 75y 20k
Layer 2	0c 60m 100y 0k
Layer 3	0c 0m 0y 0k
Layer 4	50c 30m 80y 5k

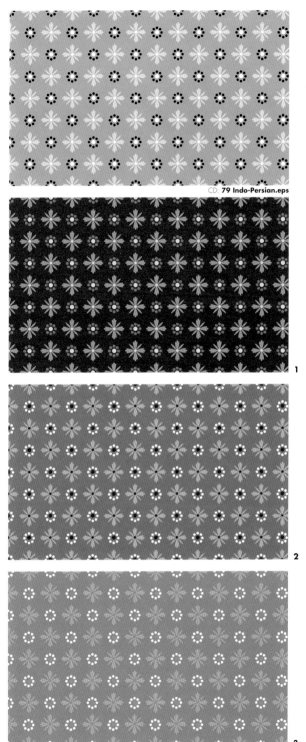

CD: **79 Indo-Persian.eps**

1

2

3

CD: **80 Indo-Persian.eps**

Indo-Persian
c.1500

Painted ornamentation was common in classic Indian architecture, and this design from a running border would have been used on a lintel or frieze. A suggestion of depth is cleverly imparted to the leafy forms by the small overlapping repeat, which would look elegant in golden yellow or orange upon a reddish-black ground.

1
Layer 1   30c 100m 80y 0k
Layer 2   0c 50m 100y 0k
Layer 3   80c 80m 40y 20k

2
Layer 1   0c 100m 30y 0k
Layer 2   70c 100m 0y 0k
Layer 3   40c 30m 20y 0k

3
Layer 1   0c 30m 70y 0k
Layer 2   60c 20m 0y 0k
Layer 3   90c 50m 10y 0k

Asian

India, c.1500

The origin of the *boteh* shape may be traced back to ancient Babylon, where it was symbolic of fertility. Its use spread to India and then, through commerce, to Britain in the eighteenth century, ultimately becoming synonymous with the small Scottish textile town of Paisley. Most recently, the motif enjoyed renewed popularity through the vivid fashion designs that typified the late 1960s.

CD: **81 Asian.eps**

1
Layer 1   75c 50m 10y 55k
Layer 2   75c 50m 10y 55k
Layer 3   0c 100m 100y 0k
Layer 4   0c 0m 50y 0k
Layer 5   0c 100m 100y 0k

2
Layer 1   75c 50m 10y 55k
Layer 2   0c 0m 0y 0k
Layer 3   100c 0m 0y 0k
Layer 4   100c 55m 0y 0k
Layer 5   100c 0m 0y 0k

3
Layer 1   0c 0m 0y 0k
Layer 2   0c 0m 100y 0k
Layer 3   0c 100m 100y 0k
Layer 4   0c 55m 0y 0k
Layer 5   0c 100m 100y 0k

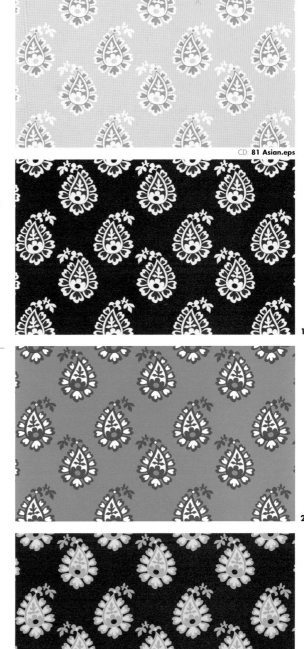

1

2

3

CD: **82 Indo-Persian.eps**

1

2

3

Indo-Persian

c.1500

In common with so many other traditions, Indian decoration derives most of its inspiration from plant life. Two distinct floral symbols combine in this decorative painted pattern, where the familiar colours of earthen red, ochre and indigo unite in agreeable harmony. Allowing the strength of the ground to recede will accentuate the feeling of space and render the resulting design airy, well spaced and uncluttered.

1
Layer 1	70c 100m 70y 0k
Layer 2	0c 10m 50y 0k
Layer 3	60c 60m 70y 0k
Layer 4	0c 60m 70y 0k

2
Layer 1	0c 70m 60y 0k
Layer 2	80c 40m 40y 0k
Layer 3	30c 40m 80y 0k
Layer 4	80c 90m 90y 0k

3
Layer 1	100c 0m 50y 0k
Layer 2	90c 100m 0m 0k
Layer 3	50c 0m 100y 0k
Layer 4	0c 100m 0y 0k

Persian
c.1500

A floral motif within a hexagon is at the heart of this geometrically sound pattern. It is unusual to find a Persian design whose colours dwell at the cooler end of the spectrum and that lacks a primary colour in all but the smallest amount, but this ornamentation has a tightness that may prove useful when used for either small- or large-scale work.

CD: **83 Persian.eps**

1

2

3

1

Layer 1	30c 10m 50y 0k
Layer 2	60c 60m 100y 0k
Layer 3	20c 80m 100y 0k
Layer 4	0c 0m 0y 0k
Layer 5	80c 50m 80y 0k

2

Layer 1	50c 80m 0y 0k
Layer 2	0c 80m 10y 0k
Layer 3	10c 40m 90y 0k
Layer 4	90c 0m 50y 0k
Layer 5	70c 90m 90y 10k

3

Layer 1	100c 100m 0y 0k
Layer 2	100c 30m 0y 0k
Layer 3	30c 100m 0y 0k
Layer 4	0c 30m 20y 0k
Layer 5	30c 20m 20y 0k

CD: **84 Asian.eps**

1

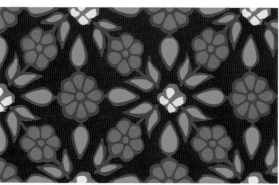

2

3

Asian

India, Traditional

There is a real sense that the petals in this timeless design have just unfurled, and that the season of renewal is upon us. In its small way, it is a work of optimism and celebration, and, like much work from India, it is informed by the highest regard for the environment. This repeat can be coloured to appear calm and soothing or bright and lively, as a project demands.

1
Layer 1   30c 0m 40y 0k
Layer 2   0c 0m 0y 100k
Layer 3   0c 100m 100y 0k
Layer 4   10c 10m 50y 0k
Layer 5   30c 20m 50y 0k

2
Layer 1   90c 0m 20y 0k
Layer 2   100c 60m 40y 0k
Layer 3   0c 80m 40y 0k
Layer 4   0c 0m 100y 0k
Layer 5   30c 20m 30y 80k

3
Layer 1   80c 60m 90y 0k
Layer 2   70c 90m 90y 10k
Layer 3   20c 50m 70y 0k
Layer 4   30c 30m 30y 10k
Layer 5   20c 40m 50y 0k

Asian
India, Traditional

A *kinkhab* is a heavy silk brocaded fabric often incorporating thread made of a precious metal. This example is from the region of Surat. The eye symbol, associated with the god Shiva, is set off well here among bold black lines. Against the golden yellow, the lighter detailing suggests the markings of a tiger – the animal also connected to this Hindu deity.

CD: **85 Asian.eps**

1
Layer 1   0c 0m 0y 100k
Layer 2   0c 15m 50y 0k
Layer 3   0c 50m 90y 0k

2
Layer 1   0c 50m 10y 0k
Layer 2   50c 0m 30y 0k
Layer 3   70c 60m 30y 50k

3
Layer 1   50c 80m 90y 0k
Layer 2   0c 100m 10y 0k
Layer 3   80c 50m 0y 0k

CD: **86 Persian.eps**

Persian
Traditional

The Persians regarded the four-headed flower symbol as something of a good-luck charm, and this simple decorative repeat, using a pattern long associated with fortune and prosperity, could hardly be more joyous and cheerful. Its buoyant, summery appearance seems remarkably modern; this pattern could just as easily have come from a 1950s curtain fabric or a cotton dress print.

1

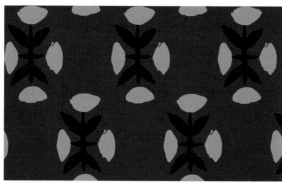

2

3

1

Layer 1	60c 20m 60y 0k
Layer 2	0c 100m 100y 0k
Layer 3	0c 20m 60y 0k

2

Layer 1	50c 100m 90y 10k
Layer 2	30c 40m 50y 0k
Layer 3	70c 80m 70y 30k

3

Layer 1	60c 80m 60y 60k
Layer 2	30c 100m 0y 0k
Layer 3	70c 0m 50y 0k

Victorian

Britain, c.1850

This decorative pattern is derived from a design intended to give the illusion of length to a small room, or height to one with a low ceiling. It is a good choice for an application that demands a strong vertical or horizontal aspect. The flowers look crisp reversed out of a darker ground, and recede when placed on a buttery yellow.

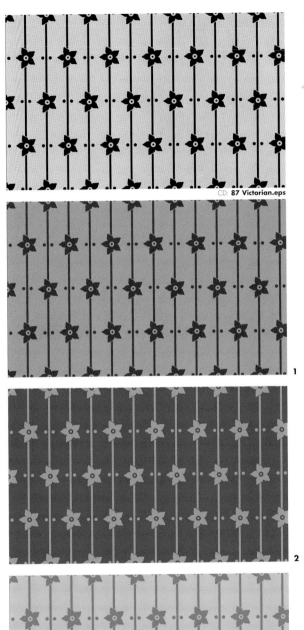

CD: **87 Victorian.eps**

1
Layer 1   70c 80m 70y 30k
Layer 2   30c 40m 50y 0k

2
Layer 1   0c 60m 30y 0k
Layer 2   100c 60m 40y 0k

3
Layer 1   100c 0m 50y 0k
Layer 2   0c 30m 100y 0k

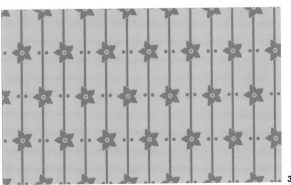

1

2

3

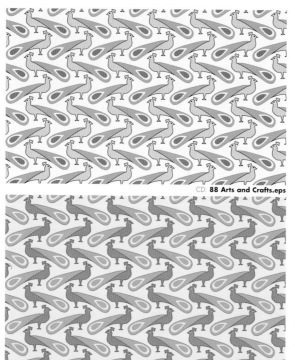

CD: **88 Arts and Crafts.eps**

1

2

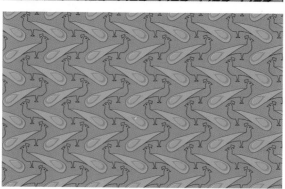

3

Arts and Crafts
Britain, c.1900

This jaunty block print was designed by the Silver Studio for the Bradford firm of Denby. The unusually playful repeat motif uses a simple colourway, its bold execution calling to mind ancient Egyptian work. A highly contrasting colour palette will lift the birds out of the ground, while a monochromatic approach will produce an effect both textural and rhythmic.

1

Layer 1	60c 0m 0y 30k
Layer 2	90c 0m 0y 50k
Layer 3	50c 60m 60y 0k
Layer 4	20c 40m 60y 0k
Layer 5	40c 20m 60y 0k
Layer 6	0c 10m 40y 0k

2

Layer 1	70c 90m 60y 10k
Layer 2	0c 0m 0y 100k
Layer 3	0c 0m 0y 100k
Layer 4	70c 100m 60y 0k
Layer 5	70c 100m 60y 0k
Layer 6	60c 50m 50y 0k

3

Layer 1	30c 60m 30y 0k
Layer 2	60c 100m 30y 0k
Layer 3	100c 60m 10y 0k
Layer 4	80c 0m 10y 0k
Layer 5	30c 40m 50y 0k
Layer 6	20c 60m 70y 0k

Modern

Britain, 2003

Blueberries feature in this design, which is given a sense of compositional tension by the way in which each fruit seems to be ready to burst out of its constraining box. As this pattern builds up over a large area, particularly on a small scale, the individual forms become less apparent and the whole assumes a pleasing abstract quality.

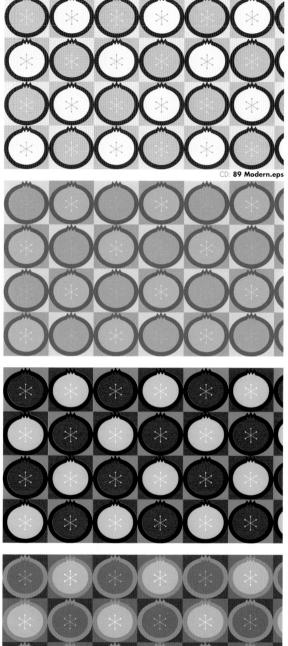

CD: **89 Modern.eps**

1

1

Layer 1	0c 20m 20y 0k
Layer 2	60c 20m 20y 0k
Layer 3	90c 60m 20y 0k
Layer 4	20c 40m 20y 0k
Layer 5	5c 20m 20y 0k

2

Layer 1	0c 0m 0y 0k
Layer 2	0c 100m 100y 0k
Layer 3	50c 0m 0y 100k
Layer 4	0c 30m 100y 0k
Layer 5	100c 0m 30y 0k

3

Layer 1	0c 0m 0y 0k
Layer 2	60c 70m 80y 0k
Layer 3	70c 30m 40y 0k
Layer 4	40c 10m 50y 0k
Layer 5	80c 80m 30y 30k

2

3

CD: **90 Modern.eps**

Modern
Britain, 2004

There is a distinctly nautical
feel to the flag-like shapes
repeated throughout this
design, which calls to mind
the interwar period of British
graphic art with its bold
directional thrust and
contrasting forms. Reversing
the triangular elements
out of a darker ground
will produce a strikingly
different pattern, while
greens and blues may
enhance its marine qualities.

1

2

1
Layer 1   0c 10m 100y 0k
Layer 2   40c 90m 0y 0k
Layer 3   0c 0m 0y 100k
Layer 4   60c 90m 0y 0k

2
Layer 1   0c 50m 10y 0k
Layer 2   80c 80m 30y 30k
Layer 3   20c 30m 40y 50k
Layer 4   0c 0m 0y 100k

3
Layer 1   100c 100m 40y 0k
Layer 2   70c 100m 0y 0k
Layer 3   0c 50m 100y 0k
Layer 4   100c 0m 0y 0k

3

Modern

Britain, 2004

Across all cultures and from the earliest times, one particular role of decorative art has been to represent celestial bodies. Venerated and celebrated by the Egyptians, the Incas, and the Celts, the sun has been portrayed more often than any other object. Restricting the colours to a range from yellow to red in this crisp modern treatment will produce a rich sunrise.

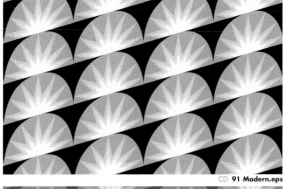

CD: **91 Modern.eps**

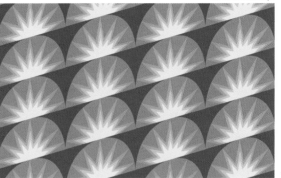

1

1

Layer 1	0c 10m 30y 0k
Layer 2	0c 30m 70y 0k
Layer 3	0c 50m 100y 0k
Layer 4	60c 40m 0y 0k
Layer 5	90c 60m 0y 0k

2

Layer 1	100c 50m 0y 0k
Layer 2	0c 50m 100y 0k
Layer 3	100c 0m 30y 0k
Layer 4	70c 100m 0y 0k
Layer 5	0c 100m 30y 0k

3

Layer 1	0c 50m 100y 0k
Layer 2	50c 100m 0y 0k
Layer 3	100c 50m 0y 0k
Layer 4	50c 50m 0y 0k
Layer 5	100c 100m 0y 0k

2

3

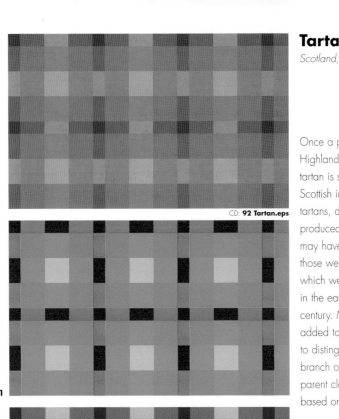

CD: **92 Tartan.eps**

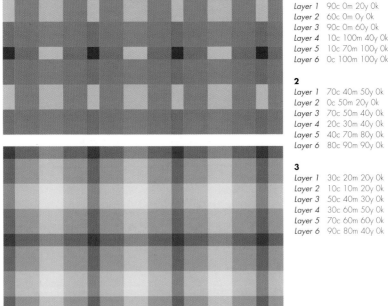

1

2

3

Tartan
Scotland, Traditional

Once a part of everyday Highland dress, Scottish tartan is synonymous with Scottish identity. The original tartans, dyed with colours produced from local plants, may have been simpler than those we recognize today, which were mostly recreated in the early nineteenth century. More detail was added to a particular design to distinguish an emerging branch of a family from its parent clan. This example is based on Agnew tartan.

1
Layer 1   90c 0m 20y 0k
Layer 2   60c 0m 0y 0k
Layer 3   90c 0m 60y 0k
Layer 4   10c 100m 40y 0k
Layer 5   10c 70m 100y 0k
Layer 6   0c 100m 100y 0k

2
Layer 1   70c 40m 50y 0k
Layer 2   0c 50m 20y 0k
Layer 3   70c 50m 40y 0k
Layer 4   20c 30m 40y 0k
Layer 5   40c 70m 80y 0k
Layer 6   80c 90m 90y 0k

3
Layer 1   30c 20m 20y 0k
Layer 2   10c 10m 20y 0k
Layer 3   50c 40m 30y 0k
Layer 4   30c 60m 50y 0k
Layer 5   70c 60m 60y 0k
Layer 6   90c 80m 40y 0k

Tartan
Scotland, Traditional

The origin of the Bruce clan can be traced back to the Norman knight Sir Robert de Brus, who accompanied William the Conqueror to England. One of his descendants was the famous Robert the Bruce, the victor at Bannockburn in 1314. Bruce tartan colours are among the most familiar; the rich red fabric crossed with bold bands is punctuated by thin contrasting yellow stripes.

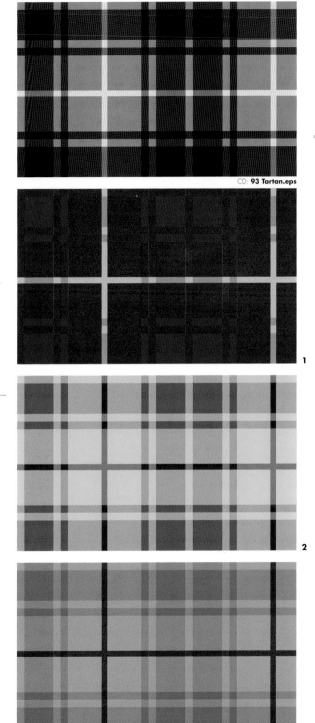

CD: **93 Tartan.eps**

1

Layer 1	70c 100m 70y 0k
Layer 2	40c 80m 70y 50k
Layer 3	10c 30m 70y 0k
Layer 4	40c 40m 100y 0k
Layer 5	0c 100m 100y 0k

2

Layer 1	30c 40m 50y 0k
Layer 2	60c 80m 90y 0k
Layer 3	80c 40m 30y 0k
Layer 4	80c 90m 100y 30k
Layer 5	30c 0m 100y 0k

3

Layer 1	40c 60m 0y 0k
Layer 2	80c 60m 20y 0k
Layer 3	0c 100m 60y 0k
Layer 4	100c 100m 0y 0k
Layer 5	50c 30m 30y 0k

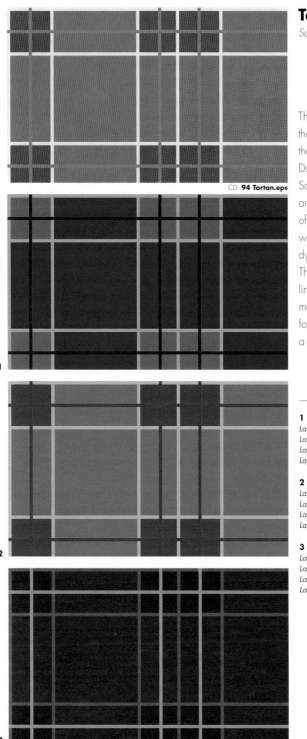

CD: **94 Tartan.eps**

Tartan
Scotland, Traditional

This pattern derives from the traditional tartan of the Colquhoun clan of Dunbartonshire in western Scotland, and the colours are immediately reminiscent of a landscape whose flora would have produced the dyes for the original fabric. The subtle tones and sparse line work here would make this a good choice for a project that demands a discreet design.

1
Layer 1   10c 40m 100y 0k
Layer 2   0c 100m 100y 0k
Layer 3   80c 50m 100y 0k
Layer 4   100c 80m 100y 0k

2
Layer 1   10c 40m 0y 0k
Layer 2   40c 90m 0y 0k
Layer 3   80c 80m 80y 0k
Layer 4   80c 50m 20y 0k

3
Layer 1   0c 90m 30y 0k
Layer 2   0c 60m 100y 0k
Layer 3   90c 100m 0y 0k
Layer 4   60c 100m 20y 0k

Oriental

Japan, Traditional

The origins of this interlocking design, called a Japanese plaid, can be traced back to the earliest times of Japanese ornamental design. The timeless device may be considered suggestive of friendship, affinity and mutual dependence. Certainly, the illusion of depth through such simple line work is remarkable, and creations such as this anticipated the work of graphic pioneers in the 1930s.

1
Layer 1   0c 20m 90y 0k
Layer 2   0c 0m 0y 100k

2
Layer 1   70c 60m 70y 30k
Layer 2   70c 30m 40y 0k

3
Layer 1   0c 50m 100y 0k
Layer 2   100c 30m 0y 0k

CD: **95 Oriental.eps**

1

2

3

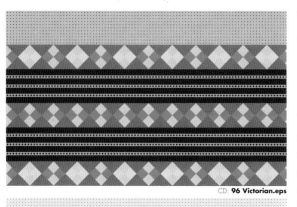

CD: **96 Victorian.eps**

Victorian
Britain, c.1870

This pattern is based on a
quilt design from the north
of England. It employs
strong vertical panels
that are given interest by
the diamond shapes and
embroidered detailing.
In contrast to much of the
fussier Victorian decorative
tendencies, the pleasant
colours and simple, well-
proportioned lines here
make for an attractive
pattern that is refreshingly
free from airs and
very versatile.

1

2

3

1

Layer 1	70c 40m 40y 0k
Layer 2	70c 40m 40y 0k
Layer 3	10c 5m 10y 0k
Layer 4	0c 50m 70y 0k
Layer 5	30c 10m 20y 0k
Layer 6	10c 5m 10y 0k
Layer 7	70c 40m 40y 0k
Layer 8	70c 40m 40y 0k

2

Layer 1	0c 60m 90y 0k
Layer 2	50c 90m 0y 0k
Layer 3	50c 90m 0y 0k
Layer 4	80c 90m 0y 0k
Layer 5	0c 80m 90y 0k
Layer 6	70c 30m 0y 0k
Layer 7	0c 60m 90y 0k
Layer 8	10c 90m 0y 0k

3

Layer 1	20c 70m 90y 0k
Layer 2	60c 100m 30y 0k
Layer 3	60c 100m 30y 0k
Layer 4	100c 100m 30y 0k
Layer 5	0c 60m 100y 0k
Layer 6	30c 100m 30y 0k
Layer 7	20c 70m 90y 0k
Layer 8	60c 100m 30y 0k

Herringbone
Traditional

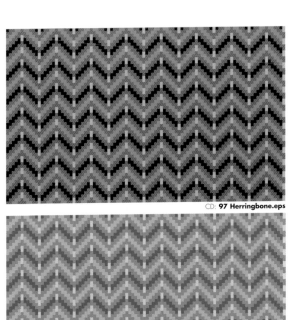

CD: **97 Herringbone.eps**

Originally developed as an embroiderer's cross-stitch, the herringbone pattern became synonymous with the classic twilled fabric with the distinctive V-shape. The term is also used to describe any pattern whose structure resembles the fish's skeleton, and can be applied to all manner of things, from necklaces to paving stone formations. The use of contrasting colour palettes will produce the boldest of zigzag designs.

1
Layer 1	60c 20m 0y 0k
Layer 2	80c 40m 0y 0k
Layer 3	0c 20m 90y 0k
Layer 4	100c 60m 0y 0k

2
Layer 1	60c 20m 50y 0k
Layer 2	30c 80m 80y 0k
Layer 3	10c 20m 40y 0k
Layer 4	80c 70m 90y 0k

3
Layer 1	80c 60m 0y 0k
Layer 2	30c 0m 90y 0k
Layer 3	6c 80m 50y 0k
Layer 4	90c 0m 30y 0k

1

2

3

Borders and Friezes

Babylonian
Assyria, c. 700 BC

CD: **98 Babylonian.eps**

Excavations at Nimroud and elsewhere along the Tigris river brought to light many ruins whose grand scale and construction may once have rivalled the greatest Egyptian pyramids. This pattern is based on a decorative architectural ornamentation unearthed in this region and displays an Egyptian influence in its subject matter. The palette incorporates the yellow, mid-blue and black common to this period.

1
Layer 1   0c 0m 0y 100k
Layer 2   0c 0m 0y 0k
Layer 3   0c 30m 90y 0k
Layer 4   70c 30m 40y 0k

2
Layer 1   80c 80m 90y 0k
Layer 2   0c 0m 0y 0k
Layer 3   40c 50m 60y 0k
Layer 4   70c 60m 80y 0k

3
Layer 1   80c 100m 20y 0k
Layer 2   0c 0m 0y 0k
Layer 3   90c 20m 0y 0k
Layer 4   40c 100m 10y 0k

1

2

3

Ancient World

Greece, c. 500 BC

Greek ornamental design was free from the worshipful symbolism found in other traditions, and most pattern work from this civilization is decoration at its most pure: ornamentation for ornamentation's sake. These decorative borders feature plant and flower devices with a reserved, formal symmetry. The simple graphic constituents will work well with many varied colour combinations.

1
Layer 1   80c 90m 90y 0k
Layer 2   0c 40m 60y 0k
Layer 3   20c 80m 70y 0k

2
Layer 1   100c 90m 0y 0k
Layer 2   100c 0m 40y 0k
Layer 3   10c 90m 0y 0k

3
Layer 1   0c 20m 90y 0k
Layer 2   70c 30m 10y 0k
Layer 3   80c 80m 80y 0k

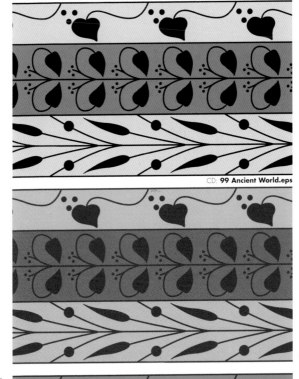

CD: **99 Ancient World.eps**

1

2

3

99

CD: **100 Ancient World.eps**

Ancient World
Greece, c. 500 BC

Natural forms such as reeds and vines informed much of Ancient Greek pattern design, and the sinuous lines of these graceful leafy representations might call to mind the work of the Art Nouveau movement. The ordered symmetry, however, is a hallmark of ornamentation from this period, and these elegant borders might be appropriate when an art or craft project calls for a discreet, mannered solution.

1
Layer 1   30c 90m 60y 0k
Layer 2   0c 20m 70y 0k
Layer 3   0c 0m 0y 100k
Layer 4   0c 40m 60y 0k

2
Layer 1   40c 100m 20y 0k
Layer 2   100c 0m 40y 0k
Layer 3   100c 100m 0y 0k
Layer 4   0c 70m 90y 0k

3
Layer 1   50c 70m 90y 0k
Layer 2   0c 50m 100y 0k
Layer 3   40c 40m 90y 0k
Layer 4   40c 100m 100y 0k

Arabian

Cairo, c. AD 900

The spread of Islam through the Middle East in the second half of the first millennium heralded a rich new design aesthetic, which, feeding on its cultural precursors, would eventually become the apogee of architectural ornamentation. This pattern is from a pavement mosaic that was constructed from marble and tile, and bears the rich colour combination of black, red and golden yellow.

1
Layer 1   90c 90m 90y 20k
Layer 2   0c 40m 90y 0k
Layer 3   0c 10m 100y 0k

2
Layer 1   60c 90m 20y 0k
Layer 2   0c 10m 30y 0k
Layer 3   60c 20m 40y 0k

3
Layer 1   100c 70m 40y 0k
Layer 2   0c 50m 40y 0k
Layer 3   60c 30m 30y 0k

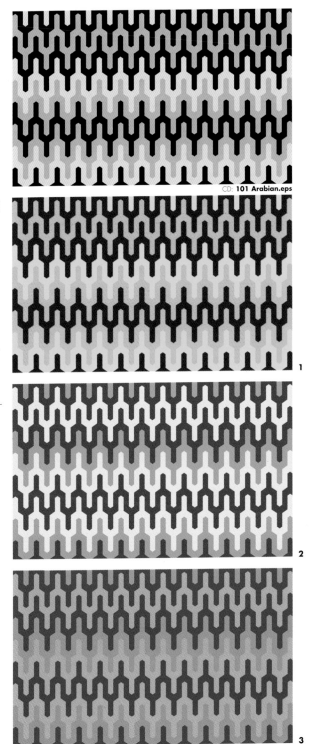

CD: **101 Arabian.eps**

1

2

3

Indo-Persian

c.1500

Borders played a key role in the vocabulary of Indian interior design, and this example from a decorative running frieze features thistle-like forms rendered soft by their sensitive, lyrical treatment. This large and detailed repeat has perfect distribution and balance, and the black ground of the original conveys a sense of luxury. It is a sumptuous, inspiring pattern.

1

2

3

1
Layer 1   0c 30m 90y 0k
Layer 2   70c 90m 70y 0k

2
Layer 1   30c 0m 100y 0k
Layer 2   80c 40m 30y 0k

3
Layer 1   0c 50m 100y 0k
Layer 2   50c 100m 30y 0k

Victorian

Britain, c.1850

This striking Victorian border pattern is notable for the way it resembles the style of the Art Deco period that followed, in terms of both choice of subject and graphic execution. The dull browns used in the original are unequivocally of their time, but this pattern can easily be vivified by using a cleaner, more modern selection of colours.

CD: **103 Victorian.eps**

1
Layer 1   10c 40m 70y 0k
Layer 2   80c 90m 90y 0k
Layer 3   0c 10m 70y 0k

2
Layer 1   50c 70m 80y 0k
Layer 2   70c 70m 0y 0k
Layer 3   0c 50m 30y 0k

3
Layer 1   80c 50m 10y 0k
Layer 2   70c 100m 0y 0k
Layer 3   50c 0m 20y 0k

1

2

3

Art Nouveau

France, 1897

CD: **104 Art Nouveau.eps**

Although blessed with the enquiring mind of a natural historian and the attention to detail of a botanist, Eugène Grasset's tendencies as an interpretative graphic artist meant that his immaculately observed subjects were often reduced to their very essence, resulting in highly stylized designs that verge on the abstract. The umbelliferous flowers here are typical of the artist at his most schematic.

1
Layer 1   0c 0m 0y 100k
Layer 2   60c 0m 20y 0k
Layer 3   0c 60m 100y 0k
Layer 4   30c 0m 40y 0k
Layer 5   0c 30m 70y 0k
Layer 6   60c 0m 20y 0k
Layer 7   40c 0m 0y 50k

2
Layer 1   100c 100m 0y 0k
Layer 2   0c 80m 20y 0k
Layer 3   0c 80m 20y 0k
Layer 4   80c 80m 20y 0k
Layer 5   70c 30m 0y 0k
Layer 6   30c 30m 30y 0k
Layer 7   80c 0m 40y 0k

3
Layer 1   80c 60m 30y 0k
Layer 2   70c 40m 40y 0k
Layer 3   80c 60m 30y 0k
Layer 4   30c 70m 40y 0k
Layer 5   40c 40m 30y 0k
Layer 6   10c 20m 30y 0k
Layer 7   20c 50m 30y 0k

Art Nouveau

France, 1897

This design taken from *La Plante et ses Applications Ornementales* is based upon a perennial woodland plant called Solomon's seal, which can be found in Eugène Grasset's native Switzerland and other northern countries. The rhythmic treatment reflects the artist's inclination to derive a sense of order from the natural world, and any number of colourways could be applied here to good effect.

CD: **105 Art Nouveau.eps**

1
Layer 1   40c 5m 50y 0k
Layer 2   0c 10m 50y 0k
Layer 3   20c 10m 40y 0k
Layer 4   90c 80m 60y 0k
Layer 5   40c 20m 50y 0k

2
Layer 1   20c 100m 0y 0k
Layer 2   100c 0m 40y 0k
Layer 3   100c 60m 10y 0k
Layer 4   100c 90m 40y 0k
Layer 5   30c 80m 90y 0k

3
Layer 1   0c 90m 50y 0k
Layer 2   10c 30m 60y 0k
Layer 3   0c 70m 90y 0k
Layer 4   70c 100m 90y 0k
Layer 5   70c 60m 90y 0k

CD: **106 Art Nouveau.eps**

Art Nouveau
France, 1897

New techniques incorporated into the glass-making process in the late nineteenth century meant that a broader range of more vibrant colours was at designers' disposal. Many of Eugène Grasset's designs from this time found their ultimate realization as glasswork, while still more patterns, such as this vine with gourds, reflect his abiding interest in the rich, saturated colours of the glass-making medium.

1

Layer 1	0c 0m 0y 100k
Layer 2	30c 20m 40y 0k
Layer 3	0c 20m 50y 0k
Layer 4	5c 50m 50y 0k
Layer 5	20c 0m 50y 0k
Layer 6	70c 30m 10y 0k

2

Layer 1	100c 60m 70y 0k
Layer 2	10c 60m 40y 0k
Layer 3	10c 10m 20y 0k
Layer 4	70c 30m 50y 0k
Layer 5	40c 20m 30y 0k
Layer 6	20c 20m 40y 0k

3

Layer 1	90c 100m 0y 0k
Layer 2	50c 60m 90y 0k
Layer 3	50c 0m 100y 0k
Layer 4	80c 0m 50y 0k
Layer 5	0c 30m 100y 0k
Layer 6	0c 100m 0y 0k

1

2

3

Art Deco

France, 1925

This border pattern may be an impression of the wheels, levers and other industrial machinery involved in mass production; alternatively, it can be perceived as an urban sunset. What is certain is that Art Deco abstraction is at its best when it intrigues and puzzles the viewer through the suggestive colourways and absorbing interplay of shapes found in designs such as this.

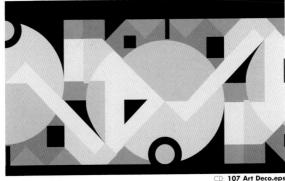

CD: **107 Art Deco.eps**

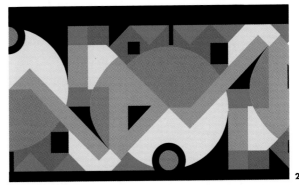

1

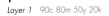

1

Layer 1	90c 80m 50y 20k
Layer 2	20c 20m 0y 0k
Layer 3	50c 40m 50y 0k
Layer 4	0c 50m 50y 0k
Layer 5	40c 20m 20y 0k
Layer 6	20c 20m 40y 0k

2

Layer 1	50c 50m 50y 100k
Layer 2	40c 70m 30y 0k
Layer 3	100c 30m 50y 0k
Layer 4	40c 0m 10y 0k
Layer 5	90c 60m 10y 0k
Layer 6	0c 70m 20y 0k

3

Layer 1	60c 80m 40y 0k
Layer 2	60c 20m 30y 0k
Layer 3	20c 20m 30y 0k
Layer 4	50c 50m 40y 0k
Layer 5	50c 50m 40y 0k
Layer 6	80c 50m 30y 0k

2

3

CD: **108 Neo-Classical.eps**

Neo-Classical
France, 1911

The influence of both Greek and Roman work can be seen in this pattern, which is derived from a tiled pavement design. Its inclusion in a twentieth-century French tile manufacturer's catalogue shows that classical styles have an enduring appeal despite the vagaries of decorative fashions, and that compositionally balanced, well-proportioned patterns will always be both popular and useful.

1

Layer 1	0c 20m 70y 0k
Layer 2	0c 50m 80y 0k
Layer 3	70c 10m 40y 0k
Layer 4	0c 0m 0y 0k
Layer 5	70c 10m 40y 0k
Layer 6	90c 100m 80y 0k

2

Layer 1	0c 40m 10y 0k
Layer 2	70c 0m 20y 0k
Layer 3	20c 30m 40y 0k
Layer 4	0c 0m 0y 0k
Layer 5	20c 30m 40y 0k
Layer 6	80c 80m 80y 0k

3

Layer 1	90c 0m 50y 0k
Layer 2	30c 40m 50y 0k
Layer 3	40c 0m 100y 0k
Layer 4	90c 90m 0y 0k
Layer 5	40c 0m 100y 0k
Layer 6	90c 90m 0y 0k

Gothic Revival

Britain, c.1880

Britain's pre-eminent Gothic Revival architect, A W N Pugin, created this wall-tile pattern – among many others – for the firm of Minton in Stoke-upon-Trent, and the influence of medieval design is clear. The standards of Victorian manufacturing were so high that countless pristine examples of such ceramics can still be found in British households, having withstood over a century's worth of domestic use.

1
Layer 1   0c 0m 0y 0k
Layer 2   40c 10m 50y 0k
Layer 3   0c 10m 50y 0k
Layer 4   40c 90m 50y 0k
Layer 5   40c 10m 50y 0k

2
Layer 1   20c 40m 60y 0k
Layer 2   0c 10m 70y 0k
Layer 3   70c 30m 50y 0k
Layer 4   80c 50m 30y 0k
Layer 5   100c 100m 0y 0k

3
Layer 1   90c 0m 20y 0k
Layer 2   0c 90m 100y 0k
Layer 3   20c 20m 30y 0k
Layer 4   0c 0m 0y 100k
Layer 5   100c 60m 0y 0k

CD: **109 Gothic Revival.eps**

1

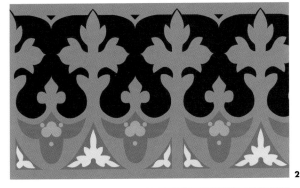

2

3

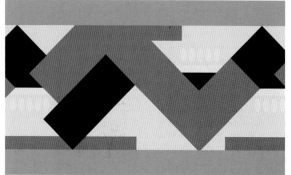

Art Deco
France, 1925

The spreading influence of Cubism and other avant-garde movements through European artistic circles was swiftly assimilated into the work of the more forward-thinking designers, and this pattern, based on one of Maurice Verneuil's *Kaleidoscope* designs, contains elements of Cubist methodology. The uncompromising palette can be seen as part of that period's artistic imperative to introduce a new vocabulary of colour.

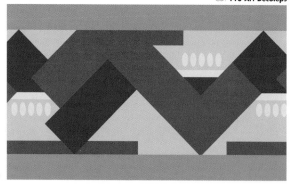

1

1
Layer 1　40c 50m 30y 0k
Layer 2　10c 10m 15y 0k
Layer 3　70c 90m 50y 0k
Layer 4　10c 90m 50y 0k
Layer 5　20c 20m 30y 0k

2
Layer 1　70c 50m 20y 0k
Layer 2　50c 30m 40y 0k
Layer 3　0c 0m 0y 100k
Layer 4　80c 20m 60y 0k
Layer 5　70c 0m 50y 0k

3
Layer 1　50c 70m 10y 0k
Layer 2　0c 60m 30y 0k
Layer 3　80c 90m 20y 0k
Layer 4　20c 100m 70y 0k
Layer 5　80c 40m 50y 0k

2

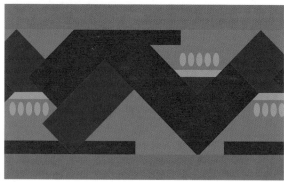

3

Art Deco

France, 1925

An illusion of perspective through the diagonal format is complemented by a sense of depth via Maurice Verneuil's typically unusual, though harmonious, choice of colours. There is, perhaps, a suggestion of animal forms within a landscape in this border pattern, and an alternative palette in which green predominates will build on this aspect and may introduce another visual dimension.

1

Layer 1	0c 60m 100y 0k
Layer 2	10c 70m 100y 0k
Layer 3	5c 40m 40y 0k
Layer 4	70c 40m 50y 0k
Layer 5	40c 20m 20y 0k
Layer 6	0c 5m 30y 0k

2

Layer 1	0c 30m 100y 0k
Layer 2	0c 100m 100y 0k
Layer 3	0c 70m 100y 0k
Layer 4	0c 100m 0y 0k
Layer 5	80c 100m 0y 0k
Layer 6	30c 100m 0y 0k

3

Layer 1	20c 10m 10y 10k
Layer 2	60c 20m 40y 0k
Layer 3	40c 20m 30y 0k
Layer 4	0c 0m 0y 100k
Layer 5	30c 40m 30y 0k
Layer 6	70c 40m 20y 0k

CD: **111 Art Deco.eps**

1

2

3

With the exception of Keith Hagan's own designs, all patterns in *The Complete Pattern Library* have been redrawn and created especially for this book. Inspiration for specific patterns is listed below; in some cases the patterns were redrawn from old fabrics or wallpapers. The Ivy Press has made every effort to credit all sources for the book; a number of the patterns included are traditional and can be seen in many sources:

page 24: Edouard Benedictus, *Variations, Quatre-Vingt-Six Motifs Décoratifs*, Paris, 1930; also reproduced in *Art Deco Designs*, Studio Editions, London 1988.

page 27: Keith Hagan.

page 38: Maurice Verneuil, *Kaleidoscope Ornements Abstraits*, Paris, 1925; also reproduced in *Abstract Art*, ABS, Studio Editions, London 1988.

page 43: Eugène Grasset, *La Plante et ses Applications Ornementales*, Brussels, 1897; also reproduced in Eugène Grasset, *Art Nouveau Floral Designs*, Studio Editions, London, 1988.

page 44: Apple, taken from a linen fabric, designed by Lindsay P. Butterfield and manufactured by G. P. & J. Baker from about 1900.

page 45: From a block-printed cotton, designed by Harry Napper and by G. P. & J. Baker from 1909.

page 46: *Etoffes et Papiers Peints*, Paris, 1924.

page 47: *Nouvelles Compositions Décoratives*, 2nd series, Paris, 1927, design by Serge Gladky; also printed in Paul Atterbury, *Art Deco Patterns*, Studio Editions, London, 1990.

pages 48, 49, 50, 51: Keith Hagan.

page 56: From a fabric designed by Georges de Feure, woven in France and sold at Bing's in 1906.

page 57: From a printed cotton from the Serpulov factory, produced in the 1920s; also reproduced in Paul Atterbury, *Art Deco Patterns*, Studio Editions, London, 1990.

page 58: E. A. Seguy, *Suggestions pour Etoffes et Tapis*, Paris, 1925; *Floreal: dessins et coloris nouveaux*, Paris, 1925.

page 59: Maurice Verneuil, *Kaleidoscope Ornements Abstraits*, Paris, 1925; also reproduced in *Abstract Art*, ABS, Studio Editions, London 1988.

page 62: From a printed silk, Stars and Stripes, designed in 1927 for the Stehli Silk Corporation; also reproduced in Madeleine Ginsberg, *The Illustrated History of Textiles*, Studio Editions, 1991.

page 63: From an endpaper design, Paul Nash, *Specimen Book of Pattern Papers*, Curwen Press, 1928; also reproduced in Paul Atterbury, *Art Deco Patterns*, Studio Editions, 1990.

page 64: Design by Serge Gladky, from *Nouvelles Compositions Décoratives*, 2nd series, Paris, 1927; also reproduced in Paul Atterbury, *Art Deco Patterns*, Studio Editions, London, 1990.

pages 66, 67, 74: Keith Hagan.

page 88: From a block-printed silk designed by Silver Studio about 1900 and printed by Stead McAlpine for the Bradford firm of Denby; also reproduced in Linda Parry, *William Morris and the Arts and Crafts Movement*, Studio Editions, London, 1989.

pages 89, 90, 91: Keith Hagan.

pages 104, 105, 106: Eugène Grasset, *La Plante et ses Applications Ornementales*, Brussels, 1897; also reproduced in Eugène Grasset, *Art Nouveau Floral Designs*, Studio Editions, London, 1988.

page 109: From wall tiles, designed by A. W. N. Pugin, c.1880.

pages 110, 111: Maurice Verneuil, *Kaleidoscope Ornements Abstraits*, Paris, 1925; also reproduced in *Abstract Art*, ABS, Studio Editions, London 1988.

Further Reading

George Audsley, Thomas Cutler, *The Grammar of Japanese Ornament* (1882).

Robert Bain, *The Clans and Tartans of Scotland* (1938).

Archibald H. Christie, *Traditional Methods of Pattern Designing* (1910).

H. Dolmetsch, *The Treasury of Ornament* (1887).

Christopher Dresser, *Studies in Design* (1876).

M. Dupont-Auberville, *Classic Textile Designs* (1877).

Madeleine Ginsburg, *The Illustrated History of Textiles* (1991).

Owen Jones, *The Grammar of Ornament* (1856).

Rexford Newcomb, *Architectural Monographs on Tiles and Tilework* (1926).

Auguste Racinet, *The Dictionary of Ornament* (1885).

Auguste Racinet, *The Encyclopedia of Ornament* (1873).

Peggy Vance, *William Morris Wallpapers* (1989).

Hans Van Lemmen, *Decorative Tiles* (1988).